The
Great Story
and the
Great
Commission

Acadia Studies in Bible and Theology

H. Daniel Zacharias, General Editor

The last several decades have witnessed dramatic developments in biblical and theological study. Full-time academics can scarcely keep up with fresh discoveries, ongoing archaeological work, new exegetical proposals, experiments in methods and hermeneutics, the rise of majority world theology, and innovative theological proposals and syntheses. For students and nonspecialists, these developments can be confusing and daunting. What has been needed is a series of succinct studies that assess these issues and present their findings in a way that students, pastors, laity, and nonspecialists will find accessible and rewarding. Acadia Studies in Bible and Theology, sponsored by Acadia Divinity College in Wolfville, Nova Scotia, and in conjunction with the college's Hayward Lectureship, constitutes such a series.

The Hayward Lectureship has brought to Acadia many distinguished scholars of Bible and theology, such as Sir Robin Barbour, James D. G. Dunn, C. Stephen Evans, Edith Humphrey, Leander Keck, Helmut Koester, Richard Longenecker, Martin Marty, Jaroslav Pelikan, John Webster, Randy Woodley, and N. T. Wright. Initiated by Lee M. McDonald and Craig A. Evans, the Acadia Studies in Bible and Theology series continues to reflect this rich heritage and foundation.

These studies are designed to guide readers through the ever more complicated maze of critical, interpretative, and theological discussion taking place today. But these studies are not introductory in nature; nor are they mere surveys. Authored by leading authorities in the field, the Acadia Studies in Bible and Theology series offers critical assessments of major issues that the church faces in the twenty-first century. Readers will gain the requisite orientation and fresh understanding of the important issues that will enable them to take part meaningfully in discussion and debate.

The
Great Story
and the
Great
Commission

PARTICIPATING
in the BIBLICAL DRAMA OF MISSION

CHRISTOPHER J. H. WRIGHT

Baker Academic
a division of Baker Publishing Group
Grand Rapids, Michigan

© 2023 by Christopher J. Wright

Published by Baker Academic
a division of Baker Publishing Group
Grand Rapids, Michigan
www.bakeracademic.com

Paperback edition published 2024
ISBN 978-1-5409-6886-9

The Library of Congress has cataloged the hardcover edition as follows:
Names: Wright, Christopher J. H., 1947– author.
Title: The great story and the great commission : participating in the biblical drama of mission / Christopher J. H. Wright.
Description: Grand Rapids, Michigan : Baker Academic, a division of Baker Publishing Group, [2023] | Series: Acadia studies in Bible and theology | Includes bibliographical references and index.
Identifiers: LCCN 2022026276 | ISBN 9781540966162 (cloth) | ISBN 9781493440238 (ebook) | ISBN 9781493440245 (pdf)
Subjects: LCSH: Mission of the church—Biblical teaching.
Classification: LCC BS2545.M54 W75 2023 | DDC 266—dc23/eng/20220801
LC record available at https://lccn.loc.gov/2022026276

The author is represented by the literary agency of Piquant Agency.

24 25 26 27 28 29 30   7 6 5 4 3 2 1

For Charlie Skrine

Hyatt Moore, *The Last Supper with Twelve Tribes*, acrylic and oil on canvas, 20 ft. ×
4 ft. 6 in., 2000. *From left to right:* Crow of Montana, Berber of North Africa, Masai
of Kenya, China, Ecuador, Afghanistan, Jesus, Ethiopia, Tzeltal of Mexico, Canela of
Brazil, Papua New Guinea, Salish of British Columbia, Mongolia.

Contents

Preface   ix

Introduction   xi

1. A Missional Hermeneutic of Scripture   1
2. The Great Story as a Drama in Seven Acts   12
3. What Does the Great Story Do?   38
4. The Great Commission and the Five Marks of Mission   60
5. Building the Church through Evangelism and Teaching   75
6. Serving Society through Compassion and Justice   87
7. The Goodness and Glory of Creation   107
8. The Goal of Creation   128
9. The Great Story, the Great Commission, and the
   Church's Mission   141

Scripture Index   153

Preface

It is never easy to condense something that one has been thinking, reading, writing, and speaking about for many years into the space of three lectures. That, however, was the task I gladly undertook when Rev. Dr. Daniel H. Zacharias invited me to deliver the Hayward Lectures at Acadia Divinity College, Nova Scotia, Canada, in October 2020. I am grateful to Danny and Acadia for that opportunity to share with the physical and online audience some biblical reflections on the nature of mission, under the overall title "The Great Story and the Great Commission: How a Missional Hermeneutic of Scripture Shapes Our Mission of Building the Church, Serving Society, and Stewarding Creation." I am similarly grateful to Baker Academic for the further opportunity of turning the lectures into this book, with considerable freedom to expand, explain, and annotate what had been so condensed in the lectures themselves, and to James Korsmo and his editorial team for many helpful suggestions and welcome improvements to the original script.

It has long been my conviction, as evidenced by some of the other books I have written on the Bible and mission, that, on the one hand, we need the whole Bible to inform our understanding of the mission of God and the mission of God's people. On the other hand, when we do use the whole Bible in the form God has given to us, it invites us to participate in the purposes of God across a wide spectrum of human life and experience and with a large horizon of biblical vision and hope. I hope this book, by sketching merely an outline of that vast breadth and depth, may enrich readers' appreciation of the great narrative drama of the Bible and help both individual believers and churches to integrate every dimension of our missional life and witness around the centrality of the biblical gospel—the good news of the kingdom of God under the lordship of Christ.

For the past two decades, it has been my great joy and privilege to belong, along with my wife, Liz, to All Souls Church, Langham Place, London, UK—ever since John Stott, rector emeritus of the church, invited me in 2001 to take on the leadership of the Langham Partnership, ministries which he had founded some thirty years earlier.[1] Having inherited the strong biblical legacy of John Stott's own ministry and teaching, All Souls maintains a theological and practical commitment to gospel-centered mission that explicitly embraces and integrates the "five marks of mission" that occupy some of the following chapters.

In appreciation of the life and fellowship of All Souls, I warmly dedicate this book to Charlie Skrine, whom we welcomed as our new rector (senior pastor) in April 2021 (which was appropriately the centenary of John Stott's birth). Early in his first year with us, Charlie preached through Paul's Letter to Titus, challenging us to see how the gospel has the power to bring about social change, provided it is taught as "the truth *that leads to godliness*" (Titus 1:1)[2] and provided that "godliness" takes the form of publicly visible good works done by Christians in all walks of life—as Paul repeatedly urges Titus to teach his people. The missional impact of the truth of the gospel, integrated with and adorned by the witness of the changed lives of those who believe and are saved by it, came across very powerfully in Charlie's preaching—and I am grateful that it has found its way into chapter 6 below.

Easter 2022

---

1. For more on these ministries, see www.langham.org.
2. Italics in biblical quotations have been added for emphasis, here and throughout the book.

Introduction

Mission is the theme of this book. And the Bible is our textbook, our source and authority.

Yet the word *mission* isn't even in the Bible! Mission is not one of those great biblical words like *faith*, for example, or *salvation* or *righteousness*. So what's the point of trying to find a *biblical* understanding of mission? But then, the word *trinity* isn't in the Bible either. And yet the Bible very clearly reveals to us the God we know as Father, Son, and Holy Spirit. We are perfectly right to talk about a biblical understanding of the Trinity, even if the word itself wasn't invented by any Bible writer.

Similarly, even if the word *mission* is not in the Bible, the Bible clearly reveals the God who drives the whole story of the universe forward with a sense of divine purpose and ultimate destiny, who also calls into existence a people who share in that divine mission, a people with an identity and role within the plan of God.[1]

And that is how I am using the word *mission* in this book—and also why I continue to use the word at all. For the fact is that *mission* has become a controversial word. Of course, there are those

---

1. See Tim Carriker, "The Bible as Text for Mission," in *Bible in Mission,* ed. Pauline Hoggarth, Fergus Macdonald, Bill Mitchell, and Knud Jørgensen, Regnum Edinburgh Centenary Series 18 (Oxford: Regnum, 2013), 29–39. This symposium has a rich collection of articles and case studies on the relationship between the Bible and mission in multiple parts of the global church.

who detest Christianity entirely because of its "missionary zeal," including aggressive proselytizing and converting people from other religions. But recently there have been some fully within the fold of evangelical Christian confession, like Michael W. Stroope,[2] who challenge the continued use of the term. This is on a variety of grounds, not merely that it is not itself a biblical word. The word was not used in the early centuries of the church, even though they were certainly *doing* what we would today call "mission," in the sense of bearing witness to their faith, in word and deed, and spreading the good news of salvation through faith in Christ farther and farther among new peoples. And we have to admit that the word does have a lot of negative baggage from the dark side of Christian missionary efforts in later centuries,[3] while in more recent times the adjective *missional* has come to be applied in so many ways as a kind of buzzword that it can be diluted almost to meaninglessness. With all those deficiencies fully recognized, I am still, however, an unrepentant advocate for the word *mission* (and its derivatives)—provided we do our best to explain clearly what it does and does not mean.

In general usage, the word *mission* can have both a broader and a narrower sense. It can refer to an overarching objective of some project or enterprise. For that reason many organizations have "mission statements," in which they state what they regard as their reason for existence and singular driving goal. In London I see even restaurant chains posting mission statements, when one might have thought that a restaurant's mission (its reason for existence) within the grand sweep of human endeavors was rather self-evident. But within that broader sense, there may also be many more specific "missions"— that is, limited goals and actions that contribute in various ways over time to achieving some overall mission.

---

2. Michael W. Stroope, *Transcending Mission: The Eclipse of a Modern Tradition* (Downers Grove, IL: IVP Academic, 2017).

3. However, it is important to recognize that the missionary expansion of the Christian church from the earliest centuries has been a complex mixture, like all things human, of good and evil. A recent and most illuminating account of this ambiguous story is by John Dickson, *Bullies and Saints: An Honest Look at the Good and Evil of Christian History* (Grand Rapids: Zondervan, 2021).

In the Second World War, for example, the Allies had an all-encompassing mission—their war aim—namely, the defeat of Nazi Germany and the liberation of the peoples that had been subjected to Nazi domination. But within that overall Allied mission, many thousands of "missions" were undertaken at multiple levels, by armed forces, secret services, espionage agents, and others, all of them aligned with and justified by the single overall mission: victory. The declared mission of the British government and their allies (to defeat Nazism) required the mobilization and participation of their people in multiple missions of many kinds.

The Bible, in this analogy, is a declaration of the single overall mission of God—to rid his whole creation of evil and create for himself a people redeemed from every tribe and nation of humanity as the population of the new creation. This declared mission of the God who governs the universe calls for the mobilization and participation of his people in multiple cultures and eras of history in manifold missions of all kinds. The mission and missions of God's people flow from and participate in the mission of God. God's plan and purpose govern ours. Or at least they should.

The Bible, then, renders to us a purposeful God and a purposeful people. And that, in essence, is what I mean by *mission* in this context. Or to put it more bluntly: In the light of the purposes of the God we meet in Scripture, what is *our* identity and mission? Who are *we* as God's people, and what are we here for? Those are questions that I hope will be better answered by the end of our journey together in these chapters. So let me outline where we will be going in the following chapters.

We need to begin by considering, in chapter 1, what is meant by "a missional hermeneutic of Scripture." This proposed way of reading the Bible has generated a lot of scholarly debate in recent years, but I will offer a survey of the main strands of biblical interpretation that go by that name.

In chapter 2 we shall explore one of those strands, the one to which I have personally devoted most attention, and that is the view that the Bible fundamentally renders to us the one overarching story of the plan and purpose of God, or what Paul calls "the whole counsel of God." I will outline that story as if it were a drama in several acts, slightly expanding the scheme proposed by Michael Goheen and Craig Bartholomew.[4]

In chapter 3 we shall explore what happens when we read the Bible in that way. And especially we shall ask: If that is God's "big story," what part in it is played by our "little stories," here and now in our own small slice of it? What does it mean to realize that we are "in the Bible," in the sense that we actually participate in the story it tells and the plan it unfolds, in the era between the resurrection and the return of Christ?

In chapter 4 we shall examine how such a "whole Bible" under-standing of the mission of God gives deep scriptural (meaning Old Testament) resonance to the so-called Great Commission and enables us to integrate all dimensions of *our* mission as God's people around the centrality of the gospel of the kingdom of God and the lordship of Christ. We shall take note of the so-called five marks of mission, simplifying them into the three broad tasks of building the *church*, serving *society*, and stewarding *creation*.

In chapters 5 and 6, we shall expand further on the first and second of those three broad areas of mission: building the church and serv-ing society. Then, in chapters 7 and 8, we shall give careful attention to the third—namely, the godly use of and care for God's creation, as a *biblical and missional issue*, not merely as an urgent contemporary one in the light of environmental and climate challenges.

Chapter 9 will draw some conclusions as to what this means for the church as a whole and for individual church members.

---

4. Craig G. Bartholomew and Michael W. Goheen, *The Drama of Scripture: Find-ing Our Place in the Biblical Story*, 2nd ed. (Grand Rapids: Baker Academic, 2014).

1

A Missional Hermeneutic of Scripture

In recent years a growing interest in reading the whole Bible from the perspective of the mission of God and the mission of God's people has generated an entire field of academic biblical studies called the "missional hermeneutics of Scripture." There is even a dedicated forum that meets annually around that topic at the esteemed Society of Biblical Literature convention, from which articles and monographs have been emerging with gratifying frequency.[1]

Broadly speaking, missional hermeneutics is a phrase that describes a method of reading and interpreting the Bible from three

1. A very helpful and informative survey of the work associated with this group and project is provided in the symposium *Reading the Bible Missionally*, ed. Michael W. Goheen, The Gospel and Our Culture Series (Grand Rapids: Eerdmans, 2016). In addition to chapters on missional readings of the Old and New Testaments and some selected biblical books and a comprehensive bibliography, this book has a usefully definitive chapter by George Hunsberger, "Mapping the Missional Hermeneutics Conversation" (45–67). Hunsberger identifies four main streams of emphasis among those currently engaged in what is loosely described as missional hermeneutics: "The Missional Direction of the Story," "The Missional Purpose of the Writings," "The Missional Locatedness of the Readers," and "The Missional Engagement with Cultures." The brief outline offered below owes a lot to Hunsberger's analysis and the stimulating reflection in the rest of the book.

major perspectives, which are complementary to one another. The Bible can be viewed as the record, the product, and the tool of God's own mission.

The Bible as the *Record* of God's Mission

This approach draws attention to *the missional framework and direction of the whole Bible story*. The way the Bible comes to us as a structured canon includes, of course, hundreds of smaller narratives, along with large quantities of text whose literary genre is not narrative at all (laws, poems, speeches, wise advice, worship songs, and so on). Nevertheless, the shape of that canon, by God's providence, starts "in the beginning" with the creation of heaven and earth in Genesis 1, and it ends with "a new heaven and a new earth" in Revelation 21–22—that is, with the renewed creation in which God will have made "all things new" and "all things in heaven and earth" will be restored and reconciled to God through the cross and resurrection of the Messiah Jesus, the towering central events of the whole story.

That grand narrative structure clearly expresses the mind and purpose of the God we meet in Scripture. Creation sprang initially from God's purposeful actions through his divine word. And the new creation will be the ultimate achievement of God's redeeming intention and action that flows through the story from beginning to end.[2] And in between, the Bible records a narrative that flows in broad chronological sequences, from the primal history of Genesis 1–11 with its gloomy portrayal of human rebellion and sin and their deathly consequences; through the ancestors of Israel and the fluctuating fortunes of the Israelites in the centuries before Christ; up to the birth, life, death, and resurrection of Jesus of Nazareth and the subsequent few decades of his followers in the first century AD; and then anticipating a future that still lies ahead of us. And this great narrative, we are constantly assured, is proceeding according to the plan and purpose of its principal character, the

---

2. Indeed, theologically (as distinct from merely chronologically), the new creation has already been "achieved" in the death and resurrection of Christ. The risen Christ is the firstborn, the firstfruits, and we who have died and risen in and with him are already "new creation" (2 Cor. 5:14–17).

Lord God, the Mighty One of Israel, the God and Father of our Lord Jesus Christ.

The Bible renders to us the story of God on mission, the mission of blessing all nations on earth and renewing the whole creation. It has become customary to present this vast narrative as consisting of four major structural segments: creation, fall, redemption, and future hope. In that shape it conforms to a very basic level of how human beings live within a "storied universe," reflected in stories of every kind that move from a good beginning, into a threatening problem or conflict, through a lengthy process to overcome the problem and resolve the conflict, to an ultimately good ending. Such stories are echoes in miniature of the actual story of the universe—the true story that the Bible tells. As Scott Sunquist puts it:

> The whole message of the Bible is the story of God's love for and relationship with his creation. It is important—both for understanding mission theology and for the message of our own missionary work—to know the story of the Scripture and be able to tell it. The Bible is God's story told through different authors, speaking different languages, in different times, using a variety of literary forms. But it is the single story of God: a public story or "open secret"; that is the story of God for all of his creation.[3]

More recently, this biblical framework has been portrayed not just as a narrative but as a drama. The Bible, argue Bartholomew and Goheen,[4] is like a vast theatrical play in six major acts (in their telling), with multiple characters playing their part (including ourselves in our section of the drama) under the overall direction of the Author—the Lord God. With many others, I have found this a helpful analogy, and I develop it somewhat in chapter 2 below.

3. Scott W. Sunquist, *Understanding Christian Mission: Participation in Suffering and Glory* (Grand Rapids: Baker Academic, 2013), 181. See also, for thorough and detailed exposition of this way of reading Scripture, Michael W. Goheen, *A Light to the Nations: The Missional Church and the Biblical Story* (Grand Rapids: Baker Academic, 2011).

4. Craig G. Bartholomew and Michael W. Goheen, *The Drama of Scripture: Finding Our Place in the Biblical Story*, 2nd ed. (Grand Rapids: Baker Academic, 2014). They intentionally build on a metaphor suggested by N. T. Wright and developed by Richard Middleton and Brian Walsh.

A missional hermeneutic, then, affirms this great, divinely directed story as the interpretive context in which we must read all the Bible's constituent parts. The meaning of the Bible's story is to be found in the plan and purpose of the Bible's God. Or to put it the other way around, understanding "the mind of God" requires understanding the Bible as the record of God's driving objective through the eons of natural history and the millennia of human history. The Bible is God's autobiography, God's story,[5] the record of God's mission. This was the growing conviction in my own theological journey that led to the writing of *The Mission of God: Unlocking the Bible's Grand Narrative*.[6] It has also shaped the approach I have taken in the commentaries I have written.[7]

Starting in this way, with the primacy of the mission of God, necessarily has its impact on how we envisage the mission of God's people within the Bible's own historical span and in the centuries since the ending of the book of Acts. Our mission flows from God's mission.

At the heart of a missional hermeneutic is the recognition that God includes a *particular people* in his plan to accomplish his cosmic work of restoration. Both the words "particular" and "people" are important. He chooses a *people*. . . . This is what distinguishes a missional hermeneutic: a people chosen by God to play a role in his purpose.

The choice of a certain people assumes a historical *particularity*—a people at a certain time and place. The direction of the biblical story is from the particular to the universal that unfolds both historically and geographically. Historically, the biblical story moves through a

---

5. This is the explicit rationale behind the ongoing Zondervan commentary series The Story of God Bible Commentary, in which I have been privileged to contribute the volume on Exodus (see note 7 below).

6. Christopher J. H. Wright, *The Mission of God: Unlocking the Bible's Grand Narrative* (Downers Grove, IL: IVP Academic, 2006).

7. Christopher J. H. Wright, *Exodus*, The Story of God Bible Commentary (Grand Rapids: Zondervan Academic, 2021); Wright, *Deuteronomy*, New International Biblical Commentary (Peabody, MA: Hendrickson, 1996; reprinted in the Understanding the Bible Commentary Series, [Grand Rapids: Baker Books, 2012]); Wright, *The Message of Jeremiah*, The Bible Speaks Today (Downers Grove, IL: IVP Academic, 2014); Wright, *The Message of Lamentations*, The Bible Speaks Today (Downers Grove, IL: IVP Academic, 2015); and Wright, *The Message of Ezekiel*, The Bible Speaks Today (Downers Grove, IL: IVP Academic, 2001).

particular means to accomplish a universal end, from one nation to all nations. Geographically, the narrative flow is from one place to every place, from a single center to many peripheries, from Jerusalem to the ends of the earth.[8]

The primary focus of most of the biblical story is particular. However, this particularized focus stands between two universal bookends: creation and consummation. The story begins with God's creation of the entire earth and the progenitors of all peoples. The story ends with the new creation and a people from all nations. The church finds its place within this movement of God's redemptive work from the particular to the universal.[9]

What then is the mission of the church? The answers to that question are legion and not without controversy. We will make our own attempt to answer it in the following chapters in a way that is, I hope, consistent with the Bible's own comprehensive scope.

The Bible as the *Product* of God's Mission

This approach draws attention to *the missional origin of the biblical documents*. The processes by which biblical texts came to be written were often profoundly missional in nature. Many of them emerged out of events or struggles or crises or conflicts in which the people of God engaged with the challenging and constantly changing task of articulating and living out their understanding of God's revelation and redemptive action in the world. Sometimes these were struggles internal to the people of God themselves; sometimes they were highly polemical struggles with competing religious claims and worldviews that surrounded them. Biblical texts often have their origin in some issue, need, controversy, or threat, which the people of God needed to address in the context of simply living as the people of God in the

8. Cf. Richard Bauckham, *Bible and Mission: Christian Witness in a Postmodern World* (Grand Rapids: Baker Academic, 2003), 13–16; and Richard Bauckham, "Mission as Hermeneutic for Scriptural Interpretation," in Goheen, *Reading the Bible Missionally*, 28–44.

9. Michael W. Goheen and Christopher J. H. Wright, "Mission and Theological Interpretation," in *A Manifesto for Theological Interpretation*, ed. Craig G. Bartholomew and Heath A. Thomas (Grand Rapids: Baker Academic, 2016), 175–76.

world. Mission, then, is not an additional interpretive reflection that we "apply" after doing our "objective" exegesis, something added as an implication of the text. Mission is in the *origin* of the text, for the text in itself is a product of mission in action, in the sense of active engagement with the issues that emerged in multiple particular contexts of Old Testament Israel or the New Testament church.

This is easily seen in the New Testament. Most of Paul's letters, for example, were written in the heat of his missionary efforts: wrestling with the scriptural and theological basis of the inclusion of the gentiles, affirming the need for Jew and gentile to accept one another in Christ and in the church as an essential outcome of the gospel itself, tackling the baffling range of new problems that assailed young churches as the gospel took root in the world of Greek polytheism and immorality and Roman imperial claims, confronting incipient heresies with clear affirmations of the supremacy and sufficiency of Jesus Christ, and so on. Similarly, the Gospels were written to explain the significance of the good news about Jesus of Nazareth, especially his death and resurrection. Confidence in these things was essential to the missionary task of the expanding church.

This missional nature of the New Testament documents, as a key to approaching the theology of the New Testament itself, is well stated by I. Howard Marshall. After making the obvious point that all the New Testament documents are concerned with Jesus of Nazareth and the repercussions of his activity, he goes on:

> It may, however, be more helpful to recognize them more specifically as the documents of a mission. The subject matter is not, as it were, Jesus in himself or God in himself but Jesus in his role as Savior and Lord. New Testament theology is essentially missionary theology. By this I mean that the documents came into being as the result of a two-part mission, first, the mission of Jesus sent by God to inaugurate his kingdom with the blessings that it brings to people and to call people to respond to it, and then the mission of his followers called to continue his work by proclaiming him as Lord and Savior, and calling people to faith and ongoing commitment to him, as a result of which his church grows. The theology springs out of this movement and is shaped by it, and in turn the theology shapes the continuing mission of the church. The primary function of the documents is thus to testify to

the gospel that is proclaimed by Jesus and his followers. Their teaching can be seen as the fuller exposition of that gospel. They are also concerned with the spiritual growth of those who are converted to the Christian faith. *They show how the church should be shaped for its mission, and they deal with those problems that form obstacles to the advancement of the mission.*[10]

Can the same thing be said about the origin of Old Testament texts? Provided we do not limit our understanding of mission to "sending out cross-cultural missionaries," I believe that it can. Many of these texts emerged out of Israel's engagement with the surrounding world in the light of the God they knew in their history and in covenantal relationship. People produced texts in relation to what they believed Yahweh, the God of Israel, had done, was doing, or would do in their world. A few examples illustrate the point.

- The Torah presents a theology of creation that stands in sharp contrast to the polytheistic creation myths of Mesopotamia and generates a very different approach to the natural world around us.

- It also records the exodus as an act of redemptive justice carried out by Yahweh, which comprehensively confronted and defeated the power of Pharaoh and all his rival claims to deity and allegiance.

- The historical narratives portray the long, bleak story of Israel's struggle with the depraved culture and idolatrous Baalism of Canaan, a struggle reflected also in the preexilic prophets. The mission of God through Israel for the world was most threatened when Israel itself succumbed to the idolatry of the nations.

- Exilic and postexilic texts emerge out of the task that the small remnant community of Israel faced as it struggled to define its continuing identity as a community of faith in the midst of successive empires of varying hostility or tolerance.

---

10. I. Howard Marshall, *New Testament Theology: Many Witnesses, One Gospel* (Downers Grove, IL: IVP Academic, 2004), 34–35 (italics added).

- Wisdom texts interact with international wisdom traditions in the surrounding cultures, but they do so with staunch monotheistic disinfectant.

- In worship and prophecy, Israelites reflect on the relationship between their God, Yahweh, and the rest of the nations—sometimes negatively, sometimes positively—and on the nature of their own role as Yahweh's elect priesthood in their midst.

This awareness of the way so many biblical texts arose in contexts of missional engagement by God's people with surrounding polytheistic cultures also embraces two of the other aspects of missional hermeneutics identified by Hunsberger—namely, *the missional locatedness of readers* and *missional engagement with cultures*.

When we read these texts as modern readers, we acknowledge that we ourselves have a particular sociocultural location and a specific missional responsibility as we wrestle with whatever challenges culture throws at us. But so did the original hearers and readers of these texts! For example, when reading the book of Jeremiah, we need to think, first of all, of the context of those who first heard *the man* Jeremiah preaching such words to them in Jerusalem in the torrid decades before 587 BC, as well as the response that they should have or could have or did or did not make to them. But we also need to think of the location and context of those who later read *the scroll* of Jeremiah as exiles in Babylon, upon whom God's judgment had fallen in fulfillment of his word through Jeremiah. How should *they* now respond? Jeremiah's letter in chapter 29 addresses precisely that question in the missional locatedness of exile and after. So a missional hermeneutic attends both to the locatedness of those in Jerusalem who *heard* the words of Jeremiah the man and to the locatedness of those in Babylon who *read* the words of Jeremiah the book—and necessarily also, of course, to the multiple sociocultural locations of those through the ages, including ourselves, who read and respond to the book in our own contexts.

In other words, the missional origin of biblical texts as, at least in part, the product of a missional engagement with surrounding cultures on behalf of God's revelatory truth and redemptive intention means that the whole task of so-called contextualization is not a new phenomenon, encountered by Western missionaries in foreign countries. It is intrinsic to the nature of the texts themselves. When we wrestle with what it means to bring the Word of God into missional engagement with culture, we are doing what the texts originally did and were meant to do.

The Bible as the *Tool* of God's Mission

This approach draws attention to *the missional aim of the biblical documents*, and it is closely related to the last point. Many of the documents in the Bible were *intended* to shape, challenge, or equip God's people for their missional task of living as God's people for the sake of God's mission in the world—a point made by I. Howard Marshall in the quotation above: "They show how the church should be shaped for its mission."

Again, this is easy to see in the New Testament, as Darrell Guder and Michael Barram have helpfully explored.[11] Paul writes his letters to encourage the small communities of believers to understand their identity in Christ and to live in the midst of the surrounding paganism of the Greco-Roman culture in a way that is consistent with the story they now inhabit—namely, the story of the one, true living God and what he has promised and accomplished in the Messiah King Jesus, as well as the glorious destiny to which that story leads. That gospel (that is, the specific claims about God and Christ that were being announced as good news) could only become believable if those who had received and believed it lived it out in transformed lives and deeds. The gospel is, as Paul puts it so succinctly, "the truth that leads to godliness," capable of transforming notorious dens of iniquity like the Crete of his times (Titus 1:1, 12).

And then the written Gospels are obvious tools of mission, for they provide the church with authentic, eyewitness accounts of the life, death, and resurrection of Jesus of Nazareth and call people to

---

11. Darrell Guder, "Biblical Formation and Discipleship," in *Treasure in Clay Jars: Patterns in Missional Faithfulness*, ed. Lois Y. Barrett, The Gospel and Our Culture Series (Grand Rapids: Eerdmans, 2004), 59–73; and Michael Barram, *Mission and Moral Reflection in Paul*, Studies in Biblical Literature 75 (Berlin: Peter Lang, 2005).

repentance and faith in him and eternal life thereby (explicitly so in John's case).

In the Old Testament era, Israel was not mandated for "centrifugal" mission—to go to the nations.[12] But they were certainly called to *live* in the midst of the nations as the people of Yahweh God, bearing witness to Yahweh's reality and sovereignty as the one, true living God of the whole earth, as well as to his character as the God of compassion, justice, love, faithfulness, truth, and so on. And in order to be that "priestly" and "holy" people for God (Exod. 19:4–6), they needed the spoken and written word that would summon them to that task and explain what it necessarily involved. That is one of the functions of Scripture, as I have written elsewhere:

> My own work on the purpose of the law in Old Testament Israel includes the observation that it was given in order to "shape" Israel into a community that would reflect the character of Yahweh, enabling them to be the public, visible exemplar of God's intention for a redeemed community of people.[13] So the legal texts can be interpreted with this sense of their "mission" within Israel's society. The mission of Israel was to be a light and blessing to the nations. The "mission" of the law was to shape Israel for that task.
>
> . . . Narratives . . . [also] functioned with powerful ethical impact, shaping the self-perception of Israel and their understanding of the norms and paradigms of what was "done" or "not done" in Israel.[14] The prophets spoke to generations of Israelites that had gotten badly "out of shape" and needed to be called back to radical repentance and conformity with the covenant requirements. The wisdom literature is most explicitly didactic in this direction, while the poetry of worship inculcates the kind of behavior, attitudes, and relationships that fit with the claims and promises of the covenant. . . .

12. On this point I differ somewhat from Walter C. Kaiser Jr., who argues that God did intend that Israel should go tell the nations about its God and the coming Messiah. I am not convinced of that. Nevertheless, there is much excellent content with which I do agree in his book *Mission in the Old Testament: Israel as a Light to the Nations*, 2nd ed. (Grand Rapids: Baker Academic, 2012).

13. Christopher J. H. Wright, *Old Testament Ethics for the People of God* (Downers Grove, IL: IVP Academic, 2004), especially chaps. 2 and 9.

14. See, e.g., Waldemar Janzen, *Old Testament Ethics: A Paradigmatic Approach* (Louisville: Westminster John Knox, 1994); and Gordon J. Wenham, *Story as Torah: Reading the Old Testament Ethically* (Edinburgh: T&T Clark, 2000).

So a missional hermeneutic asks: How did this or that particular text function to equip and shape God's people for their missional witness, and how does it continue to shape us today? The answer may include negative as well as positive dimensions, but the point is to see how Scripture, including Old Testament Scripture, functioned to enable the people of God to live out that identity and role in the midst of the world of surrounding nations.[15]

In short, then, a missional hermeneutic operates on the conviction that the whole Bible renders to us the story of God's mission through God's people in their engagement with God's world for the sake of God's purpose for the whole of God's creation.

The significance of such a comprehensive missional hermeneutic, in relation to the theme of this book, is that it compels us to engage with the *whole* Bible from this perspective—to see the whole Bible as relevant to mission (God's mission and ours), rather than basing our mission theology and practice solely upon a few "missionary texts" here and there. We can and should ask of *any* part of the Bible how and where it fits into God's great missional agenda, as well as how and where it impacts us as God's people, in whatever context in which we are called to engage in mission for God's sake and the gospel's.

---

15. Christopher J. H. Wright, "Mission and Old Testament Interpretation," in *Hearing the Old Testament: Listening for God's Address*, ed. Craig G. Bartholomew and David J. H. Beldman (Grand Rapids: Eerdmans, 2012), 185–86.

2

The Great Story as a Drama in Seven Acts

In our first chapter, we urged the need to take the Bible as a whole in our thinking about mission (or anything else, we might add!). But that raises a question: What do we think the Bible actually is? And to answer that, it might be good to consider what the Bible is *not*. I start here because it does seem to me that many Christians treat their Bibles in one or more of these ways—none of which is *wrong*, but all of which are simply not sufficient or conducive to seeing the Bible as a whole.

> The Bible is not just a book full of *promises*—though there are many, and they are very encouraging!
>
> The Bible is not just a book full of *doctrines*—for those who like big words and systematic theology.
>
> The Bible is not just a book full of *rules*—though there are some tough ones, reminders that obedience is at the heart of discipleship.

Of course, the Bible does contain all these things (and many others), but these are not by themselves what the Bible actually *is*.

Each of these approaches tends to rely on taking the Bible in small bits and pieces—whether focusing on favorite texts that give us heart-warming promises, or building a scaffolding of proof texts for each doctrine we are systematically explaining, or providing textual support for what we see as "biblical teaching" on any given ethical issue.

All of these ways of "using" the Bible have validity in their place. But they can leave us with lots of biblical *knowledge* (all useful in its own way), but without any *overall grasp* of what the Bible is all about as a whole—not seeing the forest for the trees, as they say. Or, extending that metaphor, it's like using the Bible in the same way we use a forest to extract the logs we find most useful for constructions of our own devising, yet failing to see and appreciate the forest *as a forest*, as an integrated, living organism with meaning and value *in toto* as such.

That is how I was brought up as a child and youth in Northern Ireland. There was a lot of Bible teaching, for which I am immensely grateful. I memorized verses and some whole chapters. I won Bible knowledge quizzes. I could attach Bible verses to big doctrinal words in the catechism. I knew my Bible, I thought. But it was much later that I came to see how important it is to grasp the Bible *as one whole, coherent narrative* and the implications of that for our worldview, theology, missional understanding, and practical living. It has been a transformation from knowing lots of the Bible's *content* to seeing myself as living within the Bible's *story*. The Bible has moved from being an *object* of my appreciation and study to being the *subject* of the life I live. The Bible is not so much something I think *about* as it is something I think *with*. It is not so much that I try to "apply the Bible to my life" (as if my life were the center to which the Bible has some adjectival relevance); rather, I need to apply my life to the Bible—that is, to "inhabit" its story from within.

Returning, then, to the first major section of the last chapter, the Bible comes to us in its great overarching canonical structure fundamentally as a story, a grand narrative with a beginning, middle, and end. Or better, the Bible is *the true story* of the whole universe. It begins with creation, ends with new creation, and in between tells the story of humanity in relation to God—in sin and salvation. The Bible is, as this book's title declares, *the great story*.[1]

It is also, of course, a very *complex story*, with many twists and turns (many wrong turns too), and it is a story that is told in various literary genres other than plain narrative, which need to be seen in their rightful place within that great narrative. For example, Wisdom texts are not narrative, but they do need to be understood within that part of the narrative that we call the Old Testament (the same goes for legal and prophetic texts and psalms). Similarly, the apostolic letters are not narrative but must be interpreted within the context of that part of the biblical narrative that begins when the Word became flesh and dwelt among us. The great story is the governing context for valid exegesis and interpretation of the varied texts along the way.

Furthermore, and importantly, the Bible is *our story* because

- this is the story in which we meet the one, true living God and come to know him as the God of Israel, as the God and Father of our Lord Jesus Christ, and as our God and Savior;
- this is the story that tells us who we are and why we are here as God's people on earth—that is, it is the story that generates both our identity and our mission;
- this is the story that should shape our whole Christian worldview, for we live in God's world as inhabitants of and participants in this story;
- this is the story that shows us how we are to live as God's people on earth and that gives us the resources to do so; and
- this is the story that gives us hope for the ultimate future and sends us out in mission into this fallen but redeemed-in-Christ world.

---

1. This way of reading the Bible as one whole story, and its relevance for mission, forms the basis of the symposium *Theology and Practice of Mission: God, the Church, and the Nations*, ed. Bruce Riley Ashford (Nashville: B&H, 2011). See chap. 1, "The Story of Mission: The Grand Biblical Narrative," 6–16. It is expounded in greater depth in Bruce Riley Ashford and Heath A. Thomas, *The Gospel of Our King: Bible, Worldview, and the Mission of Every Christian* (Grand Rapids: Baker Academic, 2019), chaps. 1–4.

I mentioned in the last chapter how Craig Bartholomew and Michael Goheen, building on an analogy suggested by N. T. Wright, portray the Bible as a great drama in six acts.[2] I have taken the idea and expanded it by one—making a perfect seven acts!

The idea of the Bible as a drama is, I think, a helpful analogy. Of course, there were no theaters in biblical Israel. But the Israelites did certainly have the idea that the mighty acts of God in and through them were *visible* to the nations, who are often portrayed as spectators and witnesses of the story as it proceeds, whether in salvation or judgment. The idea of the world as an open stage on which Yahweh God was at work in Israel and the nations in the great drama of history would not have been foreign to the Israelite imagination.[3] God's purposes were being played out in a way that could be seen, understood with amazement or fear or simple curiosity, and recounted again and again in longer or shorter forms.

The Bible, then, is not just a story; it is like a massive drama—an enormous play with a huge cast of actors, all playing their part in a vast narrative whose Author and Director is God himself. Like most great dramas, the drama of the Bible is divided into several "acts"— that is, major sections or stages of the story in which distinct and significant things take place as the drama moves forward. We can picture the whole Bible as a drama with seven acts.[4]

Figure 2.1 shows how we might visualize this drama through seven symbols. I owe the inspiration for these symbols to Chris Gonzalez, leader of the Missio Dei Communities, a network of churches in Phoenix, Arizona. He drew something similar on the back of an envelope for one of his church members one Sunday, to

2. Craig G. Bartholomew and Michael W. Goheen, *The Drama of Scripture: Finding Our Place in the Biblical Story*, 2nd ed. (Grand Rapids: Baker Academic, 2014).

3. I have explored the dynamic way in which the Old Testament portrays the nations as an "audience"—indeed, as applauding beneficiaries—of all that Yahweh was doing in Israel in *The Mission of God: Unlocking the Bible's Grand Narrative* (Downers Grove, IL: IVP Academic, 2006), chap. 14, "God and the Nations in Old Testament Vision."

4. It seems worth saying at this point that I am not referring here to "dispensations," as in the premillennial dispensational scheme, but simply to major chronological sequences within the overall unified and coherent drama: successive stages in the one great story.

Fig. 2.1. The Seven Acts of the Biblical Drama

1	2	3	4	5	6	7
Creation	**Rebellion**	**Promise**	**Christ**	**Mission**	**Judgment**	**New Creation**
God, humanity, earth	The fall	OT Israel	Gospel	NT church	God puts all things right	God, redeemed humanity, new heaven and earth

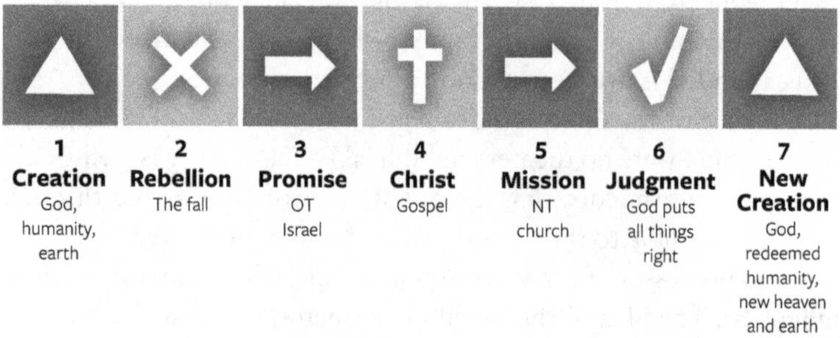

explain how the Bible can be conceptualized as a single big story.[5] I have slightly modified his originals and added number six to the sequence.

Let's look briefly at each of these seven acts of the biblical drama and seek to understand how important they are in grasping the Bible as one whole, great story. Then, when we have worked through the story in this chapter, we shall think about what happens when we read the whole Bible in this way in chapter 3. How does this way of reading the Bible affect our lives and work as Christian believers? How does it impact our mission?

Act 1: Creation

The whole drama begins when the one living and eternal God chooses to create what we call the universe—heaven and earth (see fig. 2.2). He created it "good," and he created human beings in his own image to rule and serve within his good creation on the earth.

This is like a great creation triangle of God, the earth, and humanity (which is why I made my first symbol a triangle). It is the foundation for our whole worldview as Christians. All three angles are vital for our biblical understanding, and each is related to the other two.

5. You can see Chris Gonzalez's original "True Story" symbols on the Missio Dei website: https://missiodeicommunities.com/story.

- *Yahweh God* is the Creator: the one, true living God, sovereign over his whole universe, and specifically the God to whom all creation and all humanity owe their existence, their praise and (by humans) their worship, love, and obedience.

Fig. 2.2. Act 1: Creation

1
Creation
God,
humanity,
earth

- *Human beings* were created by God in the image of God. This fact, affirmed about human beings alone among all creatures, is ontologically definitive of what it means to be human. As the image of the Creator, they are authorized to rule over the rest of the earthly creation (Gen. 1:26–28) and entrusted to serve and care for it (Gen. 2:15).
- *The earth* is "good," for God declared it to be so. It belongs to God (Ps. 24:1) and is gifted to us (Ps. 115:16). God's intention is for us to work, rest, produce, share, trade, and engage in all the activities that human life on earth makes possible.

Beneath each of these short points are vast depths of biblical truth that we cannot explore here. This first act in the drama of Scripture reveals to us who God is, what we are as humans, and where we stand in our relationship with and responsibility for the earth on which we live. And along with those theological truths go massive ethical implications. Whole books have been written on the so-called cultural mandate based on Genesis 1–2—that is, all that those chapters imply for human life on earth. The list of issues to which we must bring a moral and social perspective from this first act of the biblical drama would include the following at least:

- the nature of godly dominion over the earth and its creatures (Gen. 1:26–28) and how that requires "serving" and "keeping" (the verbs of Gen. 2:15)
- the gift of the resources of the earth and all that follows in terms of economic activity and ecological responsibility

- the implications of *all* humans being created in the image of God for the sanctity of human life, human dignity and equality within cultural diversity, and human accountability to God and one another
- the goodness and intrinsic value of human work in all its dimensions, as part of being the image of God the Worker, along with the meaning of "Sabbath" and rest
- our sexual complementarity as male and female and the role of both together in the task of ruling and serving creation, as well as the institution and nature of marriage

It is important to take this first act of the Bible story very seriously, as the foundation for all the rest. If we don't have a strong grasp of the creational *beginning* of the story and all that it means for human life, societies, and cultures, we will not have a good understanding of the *goal* of the rest of the story or of its wonderful *ending* in the new creation. Indeed, one reason for the weakness and narrowness of much that passes for "mission" in some churches and among some evangelical Christians is a woefully inadequate theology of creation. The universe in general and the earth in particular, in some people's thinking, are diminished to little more than a dispensable scaffolding for an understanding of salvation that consists largely of believers escaping from the earth altogether since it is due for cosmic incineration anyway. A theology of evacuation and obliteration! Such thinking ignores the massive significance of the Scriptures that constitute act 1 (not just Genesis 1–2 but many other creational texts in the Old Testament, such as Psalms 8, 19, 104, 148, and others). It also ignores the clear teaching of the New Testament about God's redemptive, reconciling purpose for his whole creation, not just human beings. Such texts must have an impact on our concept of mission, as we shall see in the following chapters.

Act 2: Rebellion

From the "good beginning" in act 1 of the great drama of Scripture, things go badly wrong in Genesis 3, as the "crossing out" symbol portrays (see fig. 2.3). Genesis 3 is usually referred to as "the fall," though I have never felt that to be an adequate term for what happened. We did not merely "fall" into sin, as in just accidentally tripping up. We humans *chose* to distrust God's goodness, disbelieve God's word, and disobey God's instructions. The word *rebellion* in the diagram seems more appropriate.

Fig. 2.3. Act 2: Rebellion

1	2
Creation	**Rebellion**
God, humanity, earth	The fall

Genesis 3, it is important to note, is not telling us about "the origin of evil."[6] On the contrary, we are not given any answer to our curiosity if we inquire, "How come the serpent was craftier than any other wild animal? And what does that mean? And how come this snake can talk? What's going on here?" All we can say from the text is that something is mysteriously wrong and out of place. Something that *shouldn't* happen in God's "good" creation *is* happening, and we are not told why or where it is coming from—except to say that it is not coming from God and is not initially coming from within the mind of God's human creatures themselves. Something that is other than God and external to humans has invaded the scene and is impinging on human consciousness with sinister questions. This is a story not of the *origin* of evil per se but of the *entry* of evil into human life and history.

And evil enters with devastating comprehensiveness.

Genesis 3, with its profoundly simple (yet simply profound) narrative, portrays sin and evil invading all the dimensions and relationships of human life: spiritual, intellectual, physical, and social.

- *Spiritual:* Eve is tempted to question and doubt God's truthfulness and goodness. Her trusting relationship with God is poisoned.
- *Intellectual:* She exercises her capacities of rational thought ("good for food"), aesthetic appreciation of beauty

6. That is a question that has stretched Christian theological minds and writings for a long time, with no satisfactory "answer." My own wrestling with the topic is in *The God I Don't Understand: Reflections on Tough Questions of Faith* (Grand Rapids: Zondervan, 2008), part 1, "What about Evil and Suffering?"

("pleasing to the eye"), and curiosity ("desirable for gaining wisdom"; v. 6a). All of these are good and God-given abilities in themselves. Indeed, they are highly praised in Scripture. Made in the image of God, we are authorized and encouraged to think rationally, to enjoy beauty, and to seek wisdom. The point is that all these wonderful capacities that God has given are now being exercised *in a direction that God has forbidden.* The sin lies not in the mere fact of intellectual reasoning but in using it to justify disobedience (something we have become experts at ever since).

- *Physical:* "She took some and ate it" (v. 6b).[7] Those are physical actions in the physical world, done by her own choice. Our bodies and our physical environment together are invaded by sinful choices and their consequences.

- *Social:* She "gave some to her husband, *who was with her*" (v. 6c), a detail that those of us who are men need to note. The man was not somewhere else in the garden while that conversation was taking place. He was there. He heard every word. He succumbed to the temptation just as much as she did (as God points out in v. 17).[8] So the sin that was already spiritual, intellectual, and physical became shared and social. It poisoned their relationship with each other as well as with God. Sin is relational because we are created in and for relationship as a fundamental dimension of what it means to be humans, as Genesis 1:27 and 2:18–25 express.

So one clear implication of Genesis 3 (among many, of course) is that there is no dimension of the human person that is free from

---

7. Two very simple verbs. I love the profound observation of Derek Kidner: "*She took . . . and ate:* so simple the act, so hard its undoing. God will taste poverty and death before 'take and eat' become verbs of salvation." *Genesis,* Tyndale Old Testament Commentary (Downers Grove, IL: InterVarsity, 1967), 68.

8. This is not to contradict the way Paul portrays the scene: "Adam was not deceived, but the woman was deceived and became a transgressor" (1 Tim. 2:14 ESV). Clearly both Adam and Eve sinned and became transgressors. So if that occurred because, in Eve's case, she was deceived, then in Adam's case he became a transgressor *without* being deceived by the serpent's lies. Adam sinned with his eyes open.

the presence and damaging effects of sin and evil. The doctrine of "total depravity" has been much misunderstood. It is not saying that we humans are all as bad as we possibly could be ("totally depraved" in popular usage), which is obviously not the case. Rather, it is saying that at no point are we as good as we should be. There is no part of the human person that is unaffected by sin. We are "depraved" (in the sense of fallen and sinful) in the totality of our being.

But that is not the worst of it. Genesis 4–11 goes on to show how sin not only impacts individual and relational life but also grows and escalates through the generations and centuries of history, spreads to societies and nations, leads to corruption and violence, infects all cultures, creates division and confusion among nations, and brings damage and frustration to creation. Sin has pervaded the structures of human society, hardened and entrenched as they are through historical longevity and cultural approval. "The effects of sin and the power of evil have permeated the fabric of cultural, economic, social, political and religious life, causing poverty and damaging the creation."[9]

If you are suffering from a serious illness, you need a serious and accurate diagnosis if there is to be any adequate treatment and cure. Inaccurate or inadequate diagnoses can prove fatal. Similarly, we need to understand the Bible's radical and comprehensive diagnosis of sin and evil in order to appreciate the even more radical and comprehensive scope of God's plan of redemption. The problem caused by our rebellion is vast and multifaceted. Hence, the gospel has to be as big as the problem. And the Bible shows us that—thank God—it is! Indeed, God announces his intention right from the start. The serpent and all the evil it represents will not have the last word (Gen. 3:15). And that's good news for humanity.

The gospel addresses every aspect of the consequences of sin and evil. So we need to understand that God's mission and the mission God calls us into must be broad and comprehensive. That will be our consideration in chapter 4.

9. "Statement of Faith," Tearfund, accessed November 5, 2021, https://www.tearfund.org/about-us/our-mission/statement-of-faith.

Act 3: Old Testament Promise

By Genesis 11 we have reached what seems like a dead end. We are in
a world of divided and scattered human nations living on an earth
that lies under God's curse. Lamech had hoped that his son Noah
(whose name sounds like Hebrew for "comfort") would bring an end
to the misery caused by God's curse on the ground (Gen. 5:29). Well,
after the flood we do have a kind of new beginning for the human
race, but sin and evil have certainly not been eliminated—not even
from Noah himself or from his family. So what on earth (literally)
can God do next?

God intervenes, as we move into act 3, with an amazing promise
and plan that moves the story forward in hope. That is why this act
is portrayed with the symbol of an arrow pointing forward (see fig.
2.4). The story moves on. The plot thickens.

It all begins in Genesis 12 with God's call and promise to Abraham. Over a series of encounters that span Genesis 12, 15, 17, and
18, God promises three main things to Abraham and Sarah: (1) that
they would have a son and then many descendants through him—a
great nation, no less; (2) that God would bless that nation in a pro-
tected covenant relationship; and
(3) that God would give them the
land of Canaan to dwell in. Those
three promises come to fulfillment
as the story of the Old Testament
unfolds in the next few books,
from Exodus to Joshua.

**Fig. 2.4. Act 3: Old Testament
Promise**

1	2	3
Creation	**Rebellion**	**Promise**
God,	The fall	OT
humanity,		Israel
earth		

But there was a fourth element
to God's promise to Abraham—
the bottom line, as it were. And it
is staggeringly vast. "Through [or
in] you," said God, "*all the families/nations on earth will find blessing.*" That promise, first made in Genesis 12:3 (author's translation [hereafter marked AT]), is repeated four more times in Genesis
(18:18; 22:18; 26:4; 28:14), so it is no mere afterthought. It is a fundamental declaration of God's intention, the agenda for the mission

of God for the rest of human history.[10] And what we need to see is how this Abrahamic promise that drives act 3, and indeed the rest of the biblical drama, is connected to act 1. At a simple level, it can be pictured as in figure 2.5.

Fig. 2.5. The Abrahamic Promise

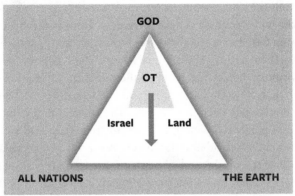

I have been using this triangle since my earliest attempts to explain the relevance of the Old Testament. It is adapted here from my *Old Testament Ethics for the People of God* (Downers Grove, IL: IVP Academic, 2004). Copyright © 2004 by Christopher J. H. Wright. Used by permission of InterVarsity Press, P.O. Box 1400, Downers Grove, IL 60515, USA. www.ivpress.com.

The outer triangle (which you might imagine colored green) portrays the creational relationships between God, humanity, and the earth that was established in act 1. But all of those relationships have been twisted, broken, and spoiled by sin in act 2. What is happening now in act 3 is that God has chosen to work redemptively on a small scale in that inner triangle (which you might imagine colored red), in order to bring blessing to the world of the outer triangle. God is still the God of all the earth and of all nations, and it is for their sake that he now initiates a project within history that will ultimately reach to that farthest extent.

Out of all nations on earth, God created and called one, Israel, to be the means of bringing blessing to the rest. And out of all the earth, he gave them one land, which would be a kind of microcosm of

10. For detailed exploration of the impact of this Abrahamic promise in the rest of the Old Testament and on into the New, see my *Mission of God*, 191–264 (chaps. 6–7).

God's promised blessing for all the earth. The Old Testament, then, is predominantly focused on this trio of relationships between God, Israel, and their land. Yahweh is the redeemer God of Israel. Israel is the covenant people of Yahweh. The land is gifted to Israel, though it remains in Yahweh's ownership (Lev. 25:23). That is the triangle of relationships that remains the primary focus of the Scriptures throughout the Old Testament era.

But the wider triangle is never forgotten. Even at the critical moment when God brings the Israelites to himself at Mount Sinai and describes them as his "special possession," God echoes the Abrahamic promise by setting them in the midst of "all nations" and insisting that "the whole earth is mine" (Exod. 19:4–6). There is a kind of double perspective or focus at work here. On the one hand, it is utterly particular: one nation in one place, as God's "special possession." On the other hand, it is as universal as God's claim on all nations in the whole earth. And that outer triangle is always there in the background and sometimes explicitly referred to in Israel's worship and prophetic texts.

When my sons were young boys, I would go to watch them play soccer. I took my camera with a long telephoto lens so that, with one eye looking through the viewfinder (it was an old, predigital SLR camera!), I could focus on one of the boys close up, filling the frame. But I kept my other eye open to watch the rest of the game, to see where the other players were, where the ball was, and so on. I was there because of my special relationship with the son in the close-up frame. But he was there because of the match going on with many other players. Similarly, "Israel is my firstborn son," said God to Pharaoh (Exod. 4:22). Naturally, therefore, most of the time the Old Testament close-up frame is filled with Israel. *But Israel is only there because God has plans for the whole earth and all nations.* God is watching the whole match (though not as a mere spectator but as its referee!).

So the key point is this: What God was doing in Old Testament Israel and their land was never intended for Israel alone, as if they were the only people to be chosen and saved. Nor is the Old Testament just a piece of ancient history that we somehow have to get through before we arrive at Jesus. Rather, God was at work in this part of the Bible story *for the sake of* all nations and the whole earth. That inner triangle was intended for the blessing and ultimate redemption of the outer triangle. To adapt a famous verse from John's Gospel (in a way John would doubtless approve), God so loved the *world* that he chose Abraham and created *Israel*. For it would be through Israel that he would give his own Son, the Messiah, for the world's salvation.

That's God's promise. That's the hope that is built into the story, from as early as the beginning of act 3.[11] That is the forward-driving dynamic of the mission of God, ever since Abraham. You could say that the mission of God throughout history, including today and tomorrow, is simply God keeping his promise to Abraham.

"All nations," said God to Abraham. "Every nation, tribe, people and language," says Revelation 7:9. Then the great story will be complete. Mission accomplished.

The "bare bones" of this long act 3 of the story include the following key moments and people:

- *God's covenant promise to Abraham:* God promises blessing for all nations.
- *The exodus:* God delivers the Israelites from slavery and oppression in Egypt, the greatest act of redemption until the cross of Christ.
- *Sinai:* God establishes his covenant with the nation through Moses and gives them his law, based on God's saving grace coming first. Obedience was (and still is) a matter of responding to God's redemptive initiative. At Sinai, too, the tabernacle was built according to the plan revealed to Moses, so that God could dwell in the midst of his people.
- *The narratives:* These tell the story of God's people from the conquest of the land under Joshua, through the era of the judges and kings (including the further covenant with the

11. Actually, the promise comes even earlier, in act 1, when God declares that the seed of the woman (i.e., a human being) will crush the head of the serpent (Gen. 3:15). Sometimes called the protoevangelium (first gospel), this verse is often seen as the first messianic prediction in Scripture, ultimately fulfilled through the victory of the man Jesus over Satan.

house of David), to the trauma of judgment in the Babylo-
nian exile and then the return to the land and establishment
of the small postexilic nation of Judah.

- *The prophets:* God's messengers highlight God's major
concerns for his people: exposing the evils of idolatry, social
injustice, abuse of economic and political power; asserting
the international sovereignty of God; holding out the future
vision of God's salvation for Israel and the nations through
God's anointed Servant-King.

- And along with this story, of course, we have *the Psalms,*
Israel's rich book of worship, and the *Wisdom literature,* in
Proverbs, Job, and Ecclesiastes.

This is a huge library of books![12] But remember: it is all "moving
forward," like a great journey, based on God's promise, and high-
lighting God's redemption, grace, and faithfulness, always pointing
toward a future destination. In the symbols above, it is represented
by a single straight arrow. But in reality it was rather more like the
Amazon River system. That is a vast and complex body of water, just
as the Old Testament is a vast and complex body of literature. But
through all its tributaries and meanderings, the Amazon is a single
water system that is moving in one direction, toward its destiny in
the Atlantic Ocean. And through all its narratives, laws, songs, and
prophecies, the Old Testament is a single story that is moving in one
direction, toward its destiny in Christ.

So, then, God's promise and Israel's hope drive the Bible story
forward through the history of Israel in the Old Testament era—act
3. Israel constantly fails to live up to their covenant commitment to
their God. But even through multiple episodes of judgment followed
by grace and restoration, God keeps the story "on course" toward
the fulfillment of his promise. Yahweh is, by definition, the God who
always keeps his promise.

---

12. I have attempted to introduce it all in a concise way that can be grasped as
a whole; see my *The Old Testament in Seven Sentences: A Small Introduction to a
Vast Topic* (Downers Grove, IL: IVP Academic, 2019).

But when would God keep his promise to Abraham about the blessing of all nations? That is the question (the "mystery," as Paul calls it in Ephesians) that is still there, alongside the promise itself, as the long era of act 3 comes to a close and as we prepare to turn a page of our Bibles through four hundred years of history and welcome Jesus in act 4.

Act 4: Christ

The promise of the Old Testament comes to fulfillment when Jesus of Nazareth is born. So the great central act of the drama of Scripture includes all that we read in the four Gospels: the conception, birth, life, teaching, atoning death, victorious resurrec-

Fig. 2.6. Act 4: Christ

1	2	3	4
Creation	Rebellion	Promise	Christ
God,	The fall	OT	Gospel
humanity,		Israel	
earth			

tion, and ascension of Messiah Jesus. The cross at the center of the seven symbols stands not just for the actual crucifixion but for the whole earthly life of Christ, from conception to ascension.

This is the heartbeat of the whole biblical drama. Acts 1–3 point toward what God accomplished in act 4, and acts 5–7 flow from it.

All we can do is summarize some of the key elements of this great central act. As with the Old Testament, every one of these deserves a chapter of its own, but we are trying to get a wide-angle overview of the great Bible story as a whole.

- *The incarnation:* The God of Israel becomes a human being and lives and walks among his people. "The Word became flesh and 'tabernacled' among us" (John 1:14 AT) is John's way of connecting the incarnation of Jesus to God's desire to dwell in the midst of his people in a tent. God "coming down" at Sinai is now surpassed by God "coming down" to a virgin's womb and Bethlehem's manger. Immanuel, God with us. The astonishing significance of this is that in this great story of Scripture, God is no longer an observer but a participant—no longer just the Director of the drama but also a visible player on the stage. "Enter God," as an Actor, "in" his own story! And he is "in it" as one of us, as a human being. That's why it is right to say that the Bible is not merely a story *about* God; it is indeed the story *of* God.

- *The kingdom of God:* Jesus announces the arrival of the reign of God that had been portrayed and anticipated in the Old Testament Scriptures. What they longed for as future is now present, in and through Christ himself. But the reign of God comes and grows in hidden ways. It is both a fact that can be announced as "good news" (God is King; Jesus is Lord) and a challenge that demands a decision (repent and enter God's reign by submitting to the lordship of Christ).

- *Jesus's life and teaching:* Here is what life in the kingdom of God looks like. The life of God's kingdom, as modeled and taught by Jesus, is radically different from the world around us. It turns most things upside down (or right way up), yet it is deeply "earthed" in real, everyday life.

- *The cross and resurrection:* Paradoxically, Jesus's life achieves its ultimate accomplishment in his atoning death and triumphant resurrection. This is, of course, the very center of the Bible's good news. God has dealt with evil, sin, and death by choosing to suffer their consequences in God's own self in the person of God the Son, thereby robbing them of power and assuring their ultimate destruction. God the Judge chooses to become the judged, as God in Christ bears our sin in himself and in our place, with the result that those who are united to Christ by faith have died and risen with him and are living here and now, by faith, in the resurrection life of the new creation.

- *The ascension and present reign of Christ:* Christ is "seated at the right hand of God"—which means "in the place of cosmic government of the nations and all history." The Gospels do not explicate the significance of the ascension much further, other than to affirm the moment when the disciples witnessed it. But texts such as Ephesians 1,

Hebrews 1, and Revelation 1 and 4–7 draw out the world-changing, cosmic importance of the simple affirmation "Jesus is Lord!"

Act 5: New Testament Mission

God's promise to Abraham must be fulfilled! The good news of what God has accomplished through his Son, Jesus, must go to all nations. That great project is launched at the end of the Gospels and beginning of Acts, after the outpouring of the Spirit of God on the followers of Jesus on the day of Pentecost. Jesus himself mandated it after his resurrection and before his ascension.

The climax of Matthew's account comes in his closing verses, which have been given the familiar title "The Great Commission" (Matt. 28:16–20). It is not, of course, the only commission or command that Jesus gave his disciples, nor is it the only biblical basis for the mission of the church (though it is sometimes elevated as if it were). But Matthew clearly intends it as the natural and logical conclusion to the story he has been telling since he introduced Jesus as the son of David (the one who was to rule the nations) and of Abraham (through whom blessing would come to all nations). His whole Gospel narrative has made it clear that Jesus of Nazareth is the one who now, after his resurrection, rightfully claims authority over all creation—none other than Yahweh, the God of Israel, himself (echoing Deut. 4:39, as we shall see in chap. 4). That being so, there is only one way forward. The world must know this great truth and the good news it brings. The nations must be discipled, baptized into relationship with the living God, and

Fig. 2.7. Act 5: Mission

1	2	3	4	5
Creation	**Rebellion**	**Promise**	**Christ**	**Mission**
God,	The fall	OT	Gospel	NT
humanity,		Israel		church
earth				

taught the obedience of faith, as Paul called it, echoing Abraham (Rom. 1:5; 16:26).

Luke records how Jesus, in the second of his Resurrection Day lectures, explicitly grounds this worldwide missional imperative in the authority of the Scriptures—meaning, of course, what we call the Old Testament. "Then he opened their minds so they could understand the Scriptures. He told them, '*This is what is written:* The Messiah will suffer and rise from the dead on the third day, and repentance for the forgiveness of sins will be preached in his name to all nations, beginning at Jerusalem. You are witnesses of these things'" (Luke 24:45–48; cf. Acts 1:1–11).

That introduction, "This is what is written," did not mean that Jesus was quoting a specific verse. Rather, he was saying: "This is the story so far, in accordance with all the Scriptures. You now know the fulfilling climax of that story, in the crucifixion and resurrection of the Messiah. But the Scriptures also reveal where the story must go next—to all nations (as God promised Abraham), and you are the ones who will bear witness to what the God of Israel has accomplished. You will be the witnesses that God called Israel to be (Isa. 43:8–10)."

So the great story of the Bible goes on!

With the launching of the mission to the gentiles, God's promise to Abraham begins to be fulfilled in ways that go beyond the individual "outsiders" who come to faith in the God of Israel in the Old Testament (like Jethro, Ruth, the widow of Zarephath, Naaman). Now multitudes from many nations are included within the expanding people of God in Messiah Jesus. The New Testament church, as a multinational community of Jews and gentiles in Christ, becomes the fulfillment of Old Testament promise and prophecy (as Paul makes very clear in Romans and Galatians). Like Old Testament Israel, disciples of Jesus are called to live as God's people *in the midst of* the nations; but we also are commanded *to go to* all nations with the good news of what God has done through Christ. Mission is to the ends of the earth till the end of the age.

And that is where we fit in the story. We participate as actors in this part of the drama of Scripture, in obedience to Christ's mandate. We live within act 5 of the Bible story, in between the resurrection of Christ and the return of Christ.

Act 6: Final Judgment

The final day of judgment will be the ultimate act of God's judgment on all sin and evil, but it is the *penultimate* act in the grand drama of Scripture—that is, the second to last. There is a wonderful "ending" to come after the final judgment, though in another sense it is a new beginning, as God himself says (Rev. 21:5). So I think the final judgment needs to be placed here as a distinct second-to-last act within the great drama of Scripture because it precedes the final resolution of the story in the new creation. Act 6 before act 7. It is the necessary prelude to that great restoration. God must put all things right before he makes all things new.

For that same reason, it is an essential part of the gospel itself: even though judgment is a terrible prospect, it is in fact good news. For the good news is that evil and Satan will not have the last word. They will finally be utterly destroyed from God's creation altogether. And, in God's ultimate justice, those who have aligned themselves with evil and have incorrigibly refused to repent will face the eternal consequences of their own sin and rejection of God. What that will mean is impossible to contemplate without horror, though we should not embellish the awful reality of hell with imaginings beyond the Bible's own deadly serious warnings. Those warnings, many from the lips of Jesus himself, insist that there is an ultimate and eternal danger to be avoided at all costs (or rather that can only be avoided at *his* cost). Perhaps the most succinctly definitive statement about the fate of the unrepentant comes from Paul when he anticipates that it will mean three things: punishment, destruction, and exclusion. "This will happen when the Lord Jesus is revealed from heaven in

Fig. 2.8. Act 6: Final Judgment

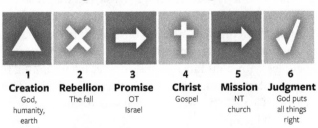

1	2	3	4	5	6
Creation	**Rebellion**	**Promise**	**Christ**	**Mission**	**Judgment**
God, humanity, earth	The fall	OT Israel	Gospel	NT church	God puts all things right

blazing fire with his powerful angels. He will punish those who do not know God and do not obey the gospel of our Lord Jesus. They will be punished with everlasting destruction and shut out from the presence of the Lord and from the glory of his might" (2 Thess. 1:7–9).

Ultimately, there will be no impunity for the incorrigibly wicked. Impunity in this life (when wrongdoers are never called to account to face justice for their deeds) is one of the scandals that exacerbates our indignation at the brutality of perpetrators and amplifies the suffering of their victims. But the Bible story tells us, as good news, that evildoers will not, as they say, "get away with it" forever. Justice will prevail—not our flawed, partial, and provisional exercise of human justice (important though that is in this fallen world), but the perfect and indisputable and irreversible justice of the Judge of all the earth.

God will ultimately deal with all wrongs and put all things right. That is what "judgment" means in the Bible. Judges in Old Testament Israel were not like judges in our modern courtrooms. They played a more active part in putting things right for those who were being wronged. Job 29 is a good description of what upright judges would do in the "gate of the city"—that is, in the public square where business was done and social issues dealt with. They got involved in sorting out broken relationships, arranging appropriate compensation or penalties, hearing the cases and complaints of one party against another, vindicating the innocent or wrongly accused, making sure those who exploited or oppressed others were restrained and punished if necessary. Putting things right. At least that's what they were supposed to do, though it is clear from the Psalms and the Prophets that they often failed.

God, however, does not and will not fail. So when God acts as *Judge*, it means God is *putting things right*. And that is something to look forward to, something to be very glad about. That is why Psalm 96:10–13 pictures all creation bursting forth in joy, because God is coming, and he is coming precisely to judge the earth and all its peoples with total fairness and justice. He is coming to put things right at last, for the whole earth, because he is the "Judge of all the earth" (Gen. 18:25). Act 6 is the ultimate "rectification" of all wrongs and all history.

So the final judgment is not something negative. As I said, it is actually an essential part of the gospel. For it is indeed good news that God will totally defeat and eradicate all evil. If this were not so, the universe would be a moral chaos with no meaning, no ultimate moral "sense." Rather, this certainty of final rectifying judgment gives us *hope* because we know that God will put all things right. That means hope for the lost, the oppressed, the violated, the wronged, the martyred—hope, indeed, for creation itself, as Paul insists in Romans 8.

Act 7: New Creation

The final act of the drama is when Christ returns to establish his kingdom. After the resurrection of the dead and the final judgment, the whole creation will be purged, cleansed, freed from all evil and sin and curse, and renewed. That is why the final symbol is, once again, the creational triangle of God, humanity, and creation—but in the glory of ultimate redemption and restoration. For, as we read in John's vision of that wonderful future, "'The old order of things has passed away.' He who was seated on the throne said, 'I am making everything new!'" (Rev. 21:4–5). This is the great biblical *hope*—using that word in its full biblical sense. That is, this is not merely something we would like to think *might* happen. This is what we confidently expect *will* happen, because of the certainty of the promises of God and the guarantee of Christ's resurrection.

Fig. 2.9. Act 7: New Creation

1	2	3	4	5	6	7
Creation	**Rebellion**	**Promise**	**Christ**	**Mission**	**Judgment**	**New Creation**
God, humanity, earth	The fall	OT Israel	Gospel	NT church	God puts all things right	God, redeemed humanity, new heaven and earth

Contrary to much popular Christian imagination (and a lot of hymns and songs), the Bible ends not with "us going up to heaven" but with God and "heaven" coming down to earth. Heaven and earth become one, so that God will dwell in the midst of his redeemed people from all nations. That is the strong message of Revelation 21. In a single verse, we hear three times that God will dwell with us, with his people. "And I heard a loud voice from the throne saying, 'Look! God's dwelling place is now among [literally "*with*"] the people, and he will dwell *with* them. They will be his people, and God himself will be *with* them and be their God'" (Rev. 21:3).

This is the ultimate "Immanuel" fulfillment: *God with us.* Not us going somewhere else to be with God but God coming here to be with us. Forever. This is the "end" of the great Bible story—but it is also a "new beginning." For after putting all things right, God promises that he will "make all things new."

In Revelation 21–22, John is drawing on the original prophecy of Isaiah 65:17–25, where God says,

> See, I will create
>   new heavens and a new earth.
> The former things will not be remembered,
>   nor will they come to mind. (Isa. 65:17)

That passage goes on with a beautiful portrait of the enjoyment of human life, family, and work, in a world free from the curses of injustice, accident, theft, and environmental harm. John transposes this into his picture of life in the new creation with no more tears, death, or pain; no more murder, idolatry, immorality, or lies; no more darkness; and above all, no more curse.

John is also drawing on the temple tradition of the Old Testament, precisely by telling us that he saw no temple in the city of God (Rev. 21:22)! The whole creation has become (again) the dwelling place of God, its Creator and Redeemer, so there will be no need for a physical building to "locate" his presence. All God's people will be serving him, for his presence will be everywhere and "they will see his face"—an incredible prospect (22:3–4)!

This climactic act of the drama of Scripture, then, is not the complete obliteration of our universe but the purging, cleansing, renewal, and restoration of creation to all that God intended it to be—not a replacement earth but a renewed earth. We will consider this and some of the questions it raises more fully in chapter 8.[13]

As we think about this last great act of the drama of Scripture, the question to ask is not when this is all going to happen. Jesus explicitly warned us not to start trying to work out dates and times (which he himself in his earthly life did not know but entrusted to his Father). Rather, the questions to ask are, Are we ready any and every day for the return of Christ? And what kind of life should we be living *now*, as we participate in the ongoing act 5 of the story, in light of all that the Bible so vividly prepares us for in acts 6 and 7?

Indeed, although in chronological "earth time" (so to speak) we are still in act 5, the Bible teaches that spiritually and theologically we inhabit act 7 already. This is a tension that we have lived in ever since the New Testament itself, or to be more precise, ever since the cross and resurrection of Jesus Christ. For in bearing the sin of the world on the cross, Jesus anticipated, in a sense, act 6. That is why he could say, before he died, that the Holy Spirit would convict the world of judgment, "because the prince of this world now stands condemned" (John 16:11). Satan's decisive defeat happened at the cross, though his final destruction awaits Revelation 20. And Christ's bodily resurrection was the dawn of the new creation, of which he is the firstfruits (1 Cor. 15:20) or the firstborn (Rev. 1:5). And, as Paul puts it, through our union with Christ, we also have died with Christ and been raised with him, and we share in his ascended reign (Eph. 2:4–6; Col. 2:20–3:4). As the apostle graphically exclaims elsewhere,

13. I have discussed this in greater detail, with a view to finding some simple biblical clarity in the midst of the many weird and obscure theories that surround the whole topic of "the end times," in *The God I Don't Understand*, part 4, "What about the End of the World?" See also, for a very helpful and thoroughly biblical understanding of what the Bible teaches about the future of creation, N. T. Wright, *Surprised by Hope: Rethinking Heaven, the Resurrection, and the Mission of the Church* (New York: HarperOne, 2008), and J. Richard Middleton, *A New Heaven and a New Earth: Reclaiming Biblical Eschatology* (Grand Rapids: Baker Academic, 2014).

For Christ's love compels us, because we are convinced that one died for all, and therefore all died. And he died for all, that those who live should no longer live for themselves but for him who died for them and was raised again. So from now on we regard no one from a worldly point of view. Though we once regarded Christ in this way, we do so no longer. Therefore, if anyone is in Christ, *the new creation has come: The old has gone, the new is here!* (2 Cor. 5:14–17)[14]

We live, therefore, in this great "overlap" within the Bible's narrative, an overlap that creates the familiar "already but not yet" of the Christian life.

- *Already:* From the point of view of God's eternal plan and his accomplishment through Christ, new creation began when God raised Jesus from the dead, and we live as those who, by faith, are risen with him and are created anew for life in the new creation. We are already living in the new age.
- *Not yet:* But from the point of view of this fallen world and its ongoing temporal story, we live still in act 5, waiting with longing and hope for our Lord to return and serving the mission of God until he does. We are living still in this old age. More on this in our next chapter.

So there we have it. That is the Bible as one whole, great story. That is the grand narrative that embraces the whole canon of Scripture, with all its different blocks and kinds of literature. That is the great drama of Scripture, with its cast of thousands and its sequence of acts, a drama in which we ourselves are participating.

And that, I believe, is what Paul means when he talks about the "whole counsel of God" (Acts 20:27 ESV) or the "will" of God for "all things in heaven and on earth" (Eph. 1:9–10). Not that Paul was thinking of a Greek drama in seven acts! But certainly Paul would have meant the whole story of Old Testament Israel (which he could summarize in a few sentences, as in Acts 13:17–22)—the story that

---

14. Notice how Rev. 21 echoes such phrases.

climaxed in the death and resurrection of Messiah Jesus, through which God has inaugurated the new creation already in the womb of this groaning old creation. It is the whole Bible story of past memory and future hope, grounded in the God of Israel.

This is the story that renders to us "the mission of God," as we saw in chapter 1. This is God's great eternal purpose that drives the whole drama of Scripture forward to its glorious ultimate goal.

3

What Does the Great Story Do?

In chapter 1 we inquired about what is meant by a missional hermeneutic of the Bible. And one of the ways in which that term is used
is to draw attention to the overall narrative structure of the Bible
in relation to the mission of God. The Bible is the story of God's
engagement in history through God's own people for God's redemptive purposes.

But the Bible is not just the *record* of God's mission; it is also the
product of God's mission. We have our Bibles because God actually
did what God planned and promised according to the Bible itself.
God spoke and God acted in multiple ways, both in the centuries of
Old Testament Israel and then in the decades of the New Testament
era. And God made sure that people wrote things down so that his
plans and purpose and accomplishments would be remembered and
known and learned and taught for all generations to come. That
need for the "mighty acts of God" to be recorded and proclaimed to
engender faith and obedience goes right back to the Old Testament
itself, of course, and it is reiterated by Luke and John when they
give the reason for writing their Gospels and by Paul and Peter for
their letters.

So the very *existence* of the Bible, in the amazing form we have it, is a proof of God's mission, through history and on into eternity. We read our Bibles to ground our faith in the certainty of what God has done in the past and to guarantee our hope in God's future. And that is why it is so important to read the Bible *as a whole*, especially as one whole, great story.

Then, in chapter 2, we outlined that one whole story, imagining it as a great drama in seven acts, centered and held together by act 4—the "Christ event." When we grasp the sweep and scope of that story, we can see every biblical book and each passage in its proper place within the overarching narrative of God, from creation to new creation. Whatever passage we are reading in the Bible, we should be asking, Where does this fit in the story? In which act of the drama are we here? What has come before this, and what is yet to come in the story? What did the "actors" at this point in the drama know from what God had already done or said, and what did they *not* yet know because it still lay ahead?

What happens when we read the Bible in this way? That is the question to which we turn in this chapter. If we adopt this narrative-missional hermeneutic—reading the Bible as one whole, coherent story of the mission of God—what does it do? I suggest five impacts of this approach.

A Missional Hermeneutic Challenges Us to "Inhabit" the Whole Bible Story

When my friend Chris Gonzalez tells the whole Bible story by drawing his "True Story" symbols on a flip chart or screen, he concludes by asking his hearers, "So where are *you* in this story?" The answers can be interesting. Some will immediately say, "In act 5." After all, that is the most obvious location to place oneself, given that it represents the stretch of historical time between the resurrection and the return of Christ. And somewhere in there is where you and I find ourselves.

Others, however, will look at the early symbols and see themselves there. After all, we are part of God's creation (act 1), and we are undoubtedly sinners perpetuating the reality of the fall (act 2). And that is a right instinct. In fact, we must extend it, because the truth is that, in different ways, we need to see ourselves with the eyes of faith in *every* act of the drama, even though the eyes in our heads give us direct sight of only our little slice of act 5. So theologically and spiritually, *we inhabit the whole story*, while chronologically we live and serve within act 5. The great story is *our* story, as much as it is God's story.

What will it mean, then, to see ourselves in every part of the story? **Acts 1 and 2** are easy. We know we are included among the human race, created in God's image, in Genesis 1. And we know that, like Adam and Eve in Genesis 3, we are sinners, fallen short of the glory of God, alienated from God, from one another, and from the earth itself that groans under God's curse.

Inhabiting those first two acts of the Bible story means that I live my daily life with both assurance and realism. The *assurance* is that, simply as a human being created in God's image, I have a significant responsibility to play my part in God's purposes for creation, stewarding all the gifts and resources he has invested into my life for the service of others, for the common good, and all for the glory of God. The *realism* is that I know not only that the world is a fallen place full of sin and rebellion and all the resultant brokenness and suffering but also that I too am a sinner, flawed in so many ways. So while I will certainly give "my utmost for his highest,"[1] I will not be surprised or discouraged when things never work out to perfection but always have elements that are partial and provisional. I will not give up in pessimism and despair but live by faith and hope, for these are only acts 1 and 2, and I know the rest of the story and how it will end.

What about **act 3**? In what sense can we see ourselves in the story of Old Testament Israel? First, we need to remember the reason Old Testament Israel came into existence at all: for the sake of all nations on earth (which, needless to say, includes you and me). To adapt the old spiritual "Were You There (When They Crucified My Lord)?"—Were you there when God called Abraham and made those gigantic promises to him and his descendants? Answer: yes. You and

---

1. To borrow the title of Oswald Chambers's devotional book, which was very much part of my early Christian pilgrimage.

I, whether we are gentiles or Jews, were among the "all nations" in the mind of God when he "announced the gospel in advance to Abraham: 'All nations will be blessed through you'" (Gal. 3:8). For in Christ "all nations" includes believing Jews and gentiles together. And on that basis, Paul goes on to assure those gentile Galatians that, through faith in the Messiah Jesus, they now belong to the people of Abraham. "If you belong to Christ, then you are Abraham's seed, and heirs according to the promise" (Gal. 3:29). Faith in the Son of the God of Abraham gives us a share in the people of Abraham. Act 3 is part of our story too.

Paul explains this unity of believing Jews and gentiles in Christ in much more depth in Ephesians 2–3 (using language like "heirs together," "fellow citizens," and "members" of God's own family), in Romans 4 (asserting that Abraham is the father of us all), and in Romans 9–11 (arguing that gentiles are grafted into the one olive tree). He can use the great scriptural narrative of Israel as directly relevant for warning, teaching, shaping, and encouraging Christian believers (e.g., Rom. 15:4; 1 Cor. 10; 2 Tim. 3:15–17). Peter does exactly the same in 1 Peter 2:9–12, applying a core Israel-describing text—Exodus 19:3–6—to his readers who were doubtless mixed gentile and Jewish believers. "*You*," Peter insists, "are that people, chosen by God, priestly and holy, God's special possession. You've had your exodus experience ('out of darkness into his wonderful light'). So now that you *are* the people of God, *live* as such among the nations, as Israel was called to do."[2]

"Live as such . . ." This does not mean that we live "under the law" in the same sense as Old Testament Israel. What it does mean, as Paul insists, is that the Old Testament law, the Torah as a whole, is as much a part of "all Scripture"—which is "God-breathed and . . . useful for

2. It is important to insist that this is not so-called replacement theology, or supersessionism, to use the older word—the idea that God somehow "gave up" on Israel and opted for the Christian church instead. The clear teaching of the New Testament is *not* that Christians have replaced the Jews but that Israel expanded to include the gentiles, in fulfillment of what God had promised all along in Israel's Scriptures. Gentile believers from all nations who trust in Messiah Jesus do not "replace" anybody. Rather, they are grafted into full membership of God's people Israel, into the new humanity that God has created through the cross of Christ, of believing Jews and gentiles, "all one in Messiah Jesus."

teaching, rebuking, correcting and training in righteousness, so that the servant of God may be thoroughly equipped for every good work" (2 Tim. 3:16–17)—as any other part of our Bible is. Sadly, the Old Testament is so neglected in Christian circles today that it is given no space to teach, rebuke, correct, or train us. How it *can* perform that function, in response to God's saving grace and missional purpose, has been part of my own thinking and writing for many years.[3]

It is because we share this spiritual identity in Christ in continuity with Old Testament Israel that we find it so natural to read, pray, and sing the Psalms. We know instinctively that these worship songs, even though they come from an ancient people who lived centuries before Jesus walked the earth, are not alien to us. Their God is our God. Their suffering and lament are ours. Their praise, thanksgiving, and joy are ours. Their faith, hope, and trust are ours. Their story is our story. That is the ringing message also of the great procession of faith and witness in Hebrews 11. We belong to this people and see ourselves in their part of the great Bible story, even though, of course, we no longer live in the "BC" historical and theological reality of the Old Testament.[4]

And so we proceed to the central act 4. We have already seen how Paul so unites us to Christ by faith that he can state directly that we have died, risen again, and ascended *with* Christ. This mind-boggling truth of our spiritual union with Christ has enormous implications for the life of faith, for our assurance and hope, and for our ongoing spiritual warfare in this life. We can't expound all those dimensions here, save to say that it all flows from "inhabiting" the Bible's story in such a way that we see ourselves *there*—"in" its central, climactic act of God's mighty, redeeming power.

3. See especially my *Old Testament Ethics for the People of God* (Downers Grove, IL: IVP Academic, 2004) and, more recently, my *How to Preach and Teach the Old Testament for All Its Worth* (Grand Rapids: Zondervan, 2015).

4. I make that last point to acknowledge the crucial importance, in another sense, of the transition from the era of the old covenant and the Mosaic law to the new-covenant life of the Spirit in Messiah Jesus—the change that Paul stresses in Galatians. Neither Jews nor gentiles who have come to faith in Jesus and the accomplishment of the cross are to "go back" to the arrangements that God ordained for Israel before Christ came, died, and rose again. Hebrews makes the same point in its distinctive way for Jewish believers.

But as I said earlier, act 4 includes not only the cross, resurrection, and ascension of Jesus Christ but his life and teaching also. So we do indeed see ourselves in the stories of Jesus that immediately precede that climax. We are obviously not among the original twelve disciples destined to become the apostolic foundation of the church. But we know that what Jesus taught them is directed to us also, as those who have come to believe in Christ through their message (John 17:20). We listen with the crowd to the Sermon on the Mount. We sit with Mary at the feet of Jesus. We puzzle over his challenging parables. We pray the prayer Jesus taught us. We heed his warnings and trust his promises. We are humbled as he washes our feet and commands us to follow his example. Oh yes, we are there "in" the Gospels, and it is in our response to the Jesus we meet *there* that our Christian faith is born and our life determined—for now and for eternity. And as we submit to Jesus as Lord, our lives in act 5 are governed by obedience to all that he taught and modeled in act 4.

We'll come to act 5 in a moment, but for now, how can we see ourselves in **act 6**, the day of judgment, since it hasn't arrived yet? This is where it is so important to see how our faith in Christ not only brings *the past* into the present (so that in our present lives we share in the death and resurrection of Christ in the historical past) but also brings *the future* into the present. The day of judgment (also variously called the day of the Lord or the day of Christ in the Bible) lies ahead in terms of earth time. But for us who are in Christ, we know that we will stand in the righteousness of Christ, who has borne that judgment. God's verdict has already been pronounced, so that we can know *here and now* that we are justified by God's grace through faith. The verdict of the judgment day to come has been anticipated for us, through faith in God's mercy and grace and the atoning work of Christ on the cross. We can see ourselves "there," knowing with Paul that we will be "found in him [Christ], not having a righteousness of [our] own . . . , but that which comes through faith in Christ" (Phil. 3:9 ESV). We can see ourselves "there" in that great crowd beyond number that John saw *standing* in the presence of the Lamb, sealed, redeemed, washed, and secure, in the wake of the day of God's wrath when the question had been cried out, "Who can stand?" (Rev. 6:17 ESV; see also

Rev. 6:12–7:17 more broadly). Answer: *We* can. We will—if we are in Christ.

And what about **act 7**, the new creation? Surely we are not "there" yet! Well, obviously not in terms of our earthly timeline, but yes, we *are* "there" in two senses. First of all, once again, we are "there" through our faith-union with Christ, for he certainly is already "there" in his resurrection and ascension. And so, as Hebrews puts it, "faith is the substance of things hoped for, the evidence of things not seen" (Heb. 11:1 KJV). And that faith is reinforced by the Holy Spirit's seal and guarantee of our inheritance to come (Eph. 1:13–14).

But secondly, we need to recognize that the resurrection of Christ really did change the world. That "first day of the week" was the first day of the new creation, the day when God declared that, in the person of his own Son, God himself had borne God's own full judgment on sin and evil on the cross; that Satan was defeated and faced ultimate destruction; and that, in raising Jesus from the dead, even death itself had lost its power. A new age dawned with sunrise and Son-rise on Easter morning. The age to come invaded the present evil age. We are already living in "the last days," and we have been ever since the resurrection of Jesus.

Actually, even the Old Testament believers had this sense of being able to live as though the future had already come into the present, as though the reign of God had already transformed the world into the reliability, righteousness, and rejoicing of all creation. So, for example, Psalms 96 and 98 summon God's people to celebrate something *now* that they knew lay in the *future*. But that future was already transforming the present in their worship. Advent was their perennial season, since Yahweh is the "coming" God: the God who had come so often in the past, who comes enthroned on the praises of Israel in the present in every act of worship, and who will come to put all things right in all creation and all nations.

Our diagram really needs some adjustment to try to envisage this. That triangle of the new creation, theologically speaking, embraces everything from the resurrection of Christ until he returns to finally bring this old age of sin and evil to an end, put all things right, and make all things new.

Fig. 3.1. Living Now in the Light of God's Future

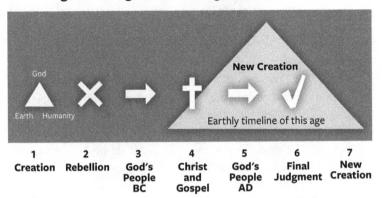

1	2	3	4	5	6	7
Creation	Rebellion	God's People BC	Christ and Gospel	God's People AD	Final Judgment	New Creation

But this affects where we see ourselves now. For we are called to say with Paul, "I have been crucified with Christ and I no longer live, but Christ lives in me. The life I now live in the body, I live by faith in the Son of God, who loved me and gave himself for me" (Gal. 2:20). We are to "see" ourselves as risen with him and living a new life altogether—the life of the new creation even while living in this age. "Since, then, you have been raised with Christ, set your hearts on things above, where Christ is, seated at the right hand of God. Set your minds on things above, not on earthly things. For you died, and your life is now hidden with Christ in God. When Christ, who is your life, appears, then you also will appear with him in glory" (Col. 3:1–4).

Notice how Paul connects the past, present, and the future in those verses. We live *now* in the light of a *past* accomplishment, a *present* spiritual reality, and a glory-filled *future* expectation. And when Paul talks about setting our hearts "on things above," he doesn't mean that we go around dreaming about heaven. He means that our life on this earth and in this age is to be governed by the standards of the kingdom of God, who reigns "above" with Christ. That is what he means also when he tells the Philippians, who were living in a renowned Roman colony where they were ruled by the laws and privileges of Roman citizenship, that "our citizenship is in heaven" (Phil. 3:20). He doesn't mean "We are all going to heaven," any more than residents of Philippi, whose citizenship was in Rome, would all go to Rome. No, he means that even though they were necessarily still living as citizens of Philippi, they must now live as citizens of heaven—that is, governed by the standards of the living God of heaven, not by the worship of the Roman emperor.

And that, of course, is a tension we continue to face as we live in this overlap period: still living in this fallen world and evil age, yet living the life of the new creation as citizens of the city of God. "If anyone is in Christ, the new creation has come: The old has gone, the new is here" (2 Cor. 5:17)—already! To put it simply: when we look at what we are told will be true in the fully realized new creation—no more depravity, murder, sexual immorality, lying, dark arts, idolatry, and so on (Rev. 21:8; 22:15)—then we have to assess and change our behavior in the here and now in the light of that future. If it won't do *then*, it won't do *now*.

And that brings us to **act 5**—where we are called to play our own part in the great drama of Scripture. In other words, reading the whole Bible as one story actually *puts us into God's story as participants in the story itself*. We are not mere spectators, not just an audience in the theater of the Bible. No, we get to be part of the story; we become actors on stage playing our part. Indeed, we are called and commissioned to join the cast of God's drama and play our part in our own generation. We are "actors" in act 5 of the drama of Scripture.

Somewhere between the first and second comings of Jesus, we find our place in history, in the Bible's own story line. And in that place, in our own generation, we have a role, we have a part to play, we have a mission to accomplish, with God and for God. "God's co-workers," as Paul amazingly put it (2 Cor. 6:1)—co-workers with the God who "inhabits" the story with us.

The Bible story is our story. We are "in the Bible"!

This has an important implication for how we think about the Bible. As I described in my personal experience at the beginning of chapter 2, the Bible is not just "an object of study." It is not just "an ancient sacred book for people of a certain religion." It is not just a "compendium of great literature" from which I can enjoyably learn so much. No, *the Bible is the story that we are in*. It is the drama in which we are actors. It is the plot in which we participate. It is, in fact, the "real world" that we inhabit.

The question we need to ask again and again is this: What story am I living in? Am I living in the world's story or God's story? Of course, we have to live "in the world," but we do not live by the story the world likes to tell. Rather, we live by the story God has given us. That's where we belong. We are in the world, but the world does not own us. We live by God's story. Or, echoing Jesus's prayer, we are sent "*into* the world" but we are not "*of* the world" (see John 17:13–18).

So, then, we inhabit the whole Bible story in all its acts by faith. And we live out our faith in practice within the act where God has placed us, act 5. How, then, should we live? That leads us to our next point. When we read the Bible as participants in God's big story, we must live in a way that is consistent with that story. To play our part in the drama of Scripture means to act in accordance with the script and the Director's instructions.

A Missional Hermeneutic Challenges Us to Live Out the Story We Are In

The apostle Paul planted churches, small communities of believers in Jesus Christ, in the midst of the colossal and overpowering Roman Empire with all its gods and its dazzling imperial ideology. They needed to know their true *identity*, now that they had come to faith in Jesus as Messiah and Lord, as the true King of the world. They were no longer (as Paul often says) "gentiles" in the sense of just living like the people around them as citizens of the idolatrous and immoral Roman Empire. But neither were most of them Jews, enjoying the legal toleration that Rome had granted to Jewish religious scruples. Who or what were they, then, these upstart *Christianoi*—"Christ fanatics," as they were nicknamed?

Through faith in Christ, Paul tells them, they had now become part of the people of God, citizens of God's country, members of God's family, the place of God's dwelling (Eph. 2:19–22). So they also needed to know the *story* that their faith in Jesus had grafted them into—that is, the scriptural story of the one true God, Creator of heaven and earth, the God of Israel, the God of Abraham and his great promise for the blessing of all nations, the God who had promised David that his son would ultimately rule the nations, the God who had come in the flesh in the person of Jesus of Nazareth, the God who had brought an end to the old world order and inaugurated the new creation in the cross and resurrection of Messiah Jesus, the God who, as Sovereign, Judge, and Savior, would bring salvation, justice, peace, and unity to the whole cosmos in a way that would far surpass the tawdry claims of imperial Rome to have done so already.

In short, they needed to know "the whole counsel [i.e., the plan and purpose] of God" (Acts 20:27 ESV), and Paul had not hesitated to spend time teaching it to them. They needed to know the biblical story in order to know this living God they had turned to (Acts 26:17–18; 1 Thess. 1:9–10) and in order to understand what this God had planned and promised and had now accomplished. And then *they must live in that story*—or, in another sense, they must live it out.

Look at what Paul prays for the new believers in Colossae, a Roman city full of gods and temples, including the worship of the emperor himself. Paul's prayer in Colossians 1:9–11 shows the kind of growth in maturity that Paul longs to see in those who have believed the gospel.

- *Paul prays for them to know God's story.* "We continually ask God to fill you with *the knowledge of his will* through all the wisdom and understanding that the Spirit gives" (v. 9). Now when Paul speaks of "the will of God," he does not mean God's guidance in his readers' personal lives. He means the same as that great explanatory text in his parallel letter to the churches in Ephesus: "the mystery of his [God's] will . . . *to bring unity to all things in heaven and on earth under Christ*" (Eph. 1:9–10). And that, as we have seen, is the whole mission of God, the ultimate goal of the whole biblical story. This is the story that stretches from creation to new creation, through all the stages that we outlined in chapter 2. And Paul wants them to *know* that purposeful plan of God thoroughly and profoundly from the Scriptures, with the help of the Holy Spirit (and his own teaching, of course, as in Acts 20:27).

- *Paul prays for them to live by God's standards.* Verse 10 gives
  the result or purpose of Paul's prayer in verse 9: "*so that
  you may live a life worthy of the Lord and please him in
  every way: bearing fruit in every good work*, growing in the
  knowledge of God." This is the practical implication—so
  characteristic of Paul's saturation in the Scriptures. There is
  a life to be lived as well as truth to be believed and teaching
  to be understood. The "will of God" that they now understand through Paul's teaching of the whole scriptural narrative, with its climax in Christ and its completion in the new
  creation, must now shape their thinking, choices, relationships, words and attitudes, behavior and habits, family, home
  and work—the whole of life, in short. They must "live a life
  worthy" of all that God has done and said and planned in
  the biblical gospel. That has to be what it means for us also
  to "inhabit" the Bible story for ourselves: we are summoned
  to live a life that is consistent with it, pleasing the God who is
  the Author, Producer, and Director of the story we are in. As
  we play our part in the great drama of Scripture, we need to
  be worthy actors on the stage.
- *Paul prays for them to prove God's strength.* He continues,
  "being strengthened with all power according to his glorious
  might so that you may have *great endurance and patience*"
  (v. 11). Paul knew firsthand that they would need exactly
  that. In view of the surrounding and overwhelming culture of
  imperial Rome, with emperor worship already beginning to
  become popular and most business deals and other social in-
  teractions happening in the context of sacrificial feasts in the
  temples of multiple gods, Christian believers who chose not
  to participate in such things would face misunderstanding
  at least and ostracism, hatred, legal and civil exclusion, possible imprisonment, and death at worst. Choosing to become
  a follower of the crucified Jesus of Nazareth as Messiah
  (and thereby forfeiting the legal protection that monotheistic Jews had long enjoyed), choosing to affirm that the risen
  and ascended Jesus is Lord (and therefore refusing to join
  in the ubiquitous salutation that "Caesar is Lord")—such

outlandish, deviant, and subversive choices could land you in serious trouble. "Becoming a Christian" was not just a matter of private, subjective belief that you could profess without any material difference in your public life, as it has so flaccidly become in our Western world. It meant signing up for suffering and persecution and an uncertain future in this life, just as it still does for vast numbers of Christ followers in many countries today. Strength, power, endurance, patience—yes, indeed; all of the above.

We are called, then, to live within the Bible's story, to live lives that are "worthy of the Lord" whose story it is.

The challenge becomes, however, that all of us already live within some other story, the story of the culture around us that shapes our worldview. So living by the Bible's story involves some degree (sometimes a very radical degree) of reshaping our existing worldview. Taking the Bible as the one whole, true story of the world, and therefore as the story that must govern our lives as Christian believers, should change the way we think about "Life, the Universe and Everything."[5]

A Missional Hermeneutic Reshapes Our Worldview

Worldviews are the lenses through which all human beings see the world around them, make sense of it, and adjust their lives accordingly. Every religion, philosophy, culture, society, and community shares some worldview or another, which may or may not be compatible with those of others. And worldviews are typically expressed and sustained by the stories people tell, or the governing story that a given culture takes as normative.[6]

5. Douglas Adams, *The Hitchhiker's Guide to the Galaxy*, 25th anniv. ed. (New York: Harmony Books, 2004), 227.

6. There are numerous books that explain what a worldview is and what it means to cultivate a biblical, Christian worldview. It is because there are so many good resources available that I have kept this section brief, with some personal reflections only. Among the most accessible such resources are James W. Sire, *The Universe Next Door: A Basic Worldview Catalog*, 6th ed. (Downers Grove, IL: IVP Academic, 2020); Brian J. Walsh and J. Richard Middleton, *The Transforming Vision: Shaping a Christian World View* (Downers Grove, IL: InterVarsity, 1984); Michael W. Goheen

Many years of engaging in a missional hermeneutic of Scripture (even when I wasn't consciously defining my approach by that phrase) eventually led to the labor of love known as *The Mission of God: Unlocking the Bible's Grand Narrative*. And the prolonged work that went into that book led me to discern some profound and subversive adjustments in my own worldview—particularly in relation to what it should mean to "inhabit" the Bible's story. As I have said, I grew up with abundant Bible knowledge injected into my youthful mind, and I was keen to "apply the Bible to my life"—and to help others do the same. I began to see that I needed to turn that approach inside out, without diminishing the value of what I'd been taught to do. Let me expand on that.

Here is how I concluded that journey, in the epilogue to *The Mission of God*.

> When we grasp that the whole Bible constitutes the coherent revelation of the mission of God, when we see this as the key that unlocks the driving purposefulness of the whole grand narrative . . . , then we find our whole worldview impacted by this vision. As has been well documented, every human worldview is an outworking of *some* narrative. We live out of the story or stories we believe to be true, the story or stories that "tell it like it is," we think. So what does it mean to live out of *this* story? Here is *The Story*, the grand universal narrative that stretches from creation to new creation, and accounts for everything in between. This is The Story that tells us where we have come from, how we got to be here, who we are, why the world is in the mess it is, how it can be (and has been) changed, and where we are ultimately going. And the whole story is predicated on the reality of this God and the mission of this God. He is the originator of the story, the teller of the story, the prime actor in the story, the planner and guide of the story's plot, the meaning of the story and its ultimate completion. He is its beginning, end and center. It is the story of the mission of God, of this God and no other.
>
> Now such an understanding of the mission of God as the very heartbeat of all reality, all creation, all history and all that yet lies ahead of us generates a distinctive worldview that is radically and

---

and Craig G. Bartholomew, *Living at the Crossroads: An Introduction to Christian Worldview* (Grand Rapids: Baker Academic, 2008).

transformingly God-centered. And my experience in wrestling with the massive contours of this Bible-sculpted, God-centered, mission-driven vision of reality, has been to find that it turns inside out and upside down some of the common ways in which we are accustomed to thinking about the Christian life and the kinds of questions we are inclined to ask. This worldview, constituted by putting the mission of God at the very center of all existence, is disturbingly subversive and it uncomfortably relativizes one's own place in the great scheme of things. It is certainly a very healthy corrective to the egocentric obsession of much Western culture—including, sadly, even Western Christian culture. It constantly forces us to open our eyes to the big picture, rather than shelter in the cosy narcissism of our own small worlds.

- We ask, "Where does God fit into the story of my life?" when the real question is where does my little life fit into this great story of God's mission.
- We want to be driven by a purpose that has been tailored just right for our own individual lives . . . , when we should be seeing the purpose of all life, including our own, wrapped up in the great mission of God for the whole of creation.
- We talk about the problems of "applying the Bible to our lives," which often means modifying the Bible somewhat adjectivally to fit into the assumed "reality" of the life we live "in the real world." What would it mean to apply our lives to the Bible instead, assuming *the Bible* to be the reality—the real story—to which *we* are called to conform ourselves?
- We wrestle with the question of how we can "make the gospel relevant to the world" (again, at least that is clearly preferable to treating it as irrelevant). But in *this* Story, God is about the business of transforming the world to fit the shape of the gospel.
- We wonder whether and how the care of creation, for example, might fit into *our* concept and practice of mission, when *this* Story challenges us to ask whether our lives, lived on God's earth and under God's gaze, are aligned with, or horrendously misaligned with, God's mission that stretches from creation to cosmic transformation and the arrival of a new heaven and new earth.
- We argue about what can legitimately be included in the mission God expects from the church, when we should ask

what kind of church God expects for his mission in all its comprehensive fullness.

- I may wonder what kind of mission God has for *me*, when I should ask what kind of me God wants for *his* mission.

The only concept of mission into which God fits is the one of which he is the beginning, the center and the end (to paraphrase what Lesslie Newbigin once said about the resurrection).[7] And the only access that we have to that mission of God is given to us in the Bible. This is the grand narrative that is unlocked when we turn the hermeneutical key of reading all the Scriptures in the light of the mission of God.[8]

A Missional Hermeneutic Governs Our Doctrinal Theology

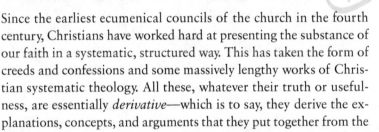

Since the earliest ecumenical councils of the church in the fourth century, Christians have worked hard at presenting the substance of our faith in a systematic, structured way. This has taken the form of creeds and confessions and some massively lengthy works of Christian systematic theology. All these, whatever their truth or usefulness, are essentially *derivative*—which is to say, they derive the explanations, concepts, and arguments that they put together from the Bible, which remains the sole authoritative revelation of and from God himself. And it is the Bible's own grand story that provides the framework and substance for the work of systematic theology.[9] Here are some examples:

- The doctrine of *God* seeks to summarize and express what we learn from the Bible about the God who is the main

7. "Indeed, the simple truth is that the resurrection cannot be accommodated in any way of understanding the world except one of which it is the starting point." Lesslie Newbigin, *Truth to Tell: The Gospel as Public Truth* (London: SPCK, 1991), 11.

8. Christopher J. H. Wright, *The Mission of God: Unlocking the Bible's Grand Narrative* (Downers Grove, IL: IVP Academic, 2006), 533–34. Copyright © 2006 by Christopher J. H. Wright. Used by permission of InterVarsity Press, P.O. Box 1400, Downers Grove, IL 60515, USA. www.ivpress.com.

9. A helpful survey of how some key doctrines in our systematic theology relate to mission is provided by Bruce Riley Ashford, "A Theologically Driven Missiology," in *Theology and Practice of Mission: God, the Church, and the Nations*, ed. Bruce Riley Ashford (Nashville: B&H, 2011), 294–318.

character in its dramatic narrative. The living God reveals himself and all his "attributes" through what he does and says in the course of it.

- The doctrine of *humanity* starts from act 1 but rapidly takes act 2 into account, and then it builds on what we learn about human nature from the narratives in act 3, along with Israel's worship and wisdom.
- *Christology* formulates not only what we find in the Gospels in act 4 but takes on board all that is prepared in advance for the birth of Christ in the Old Testament—and, indeed, what it means to recognize Jesus of Nazareth as the eternal Son of God through whom and for whom all things were created, as the "ruler of the kings of the earth" now (Rev. 1:5), and as the crucified and risen Lamb on the throne of the new creation.
- The doctrines of *grace and salvation* draw on the whole story, with its radical diagnosis of sin and then the promises of Yahweh, the gracious and saving God, that breathe through the Old Testament, reach fulfillment in the New, and explain how the good news of what God has accomplished in Christ can be received by sinners by grace through faith for eternal life.
- *Ecclesiology* binds together what the Bible affirms about the identity and mission of God's people through the whole story from Abraham in act 3 to Christ and Pentecost in acts 4 and 5, as well as the eternal future of the church as the bride of Christ and dwelling place of the Lord in the new creation of act 7.
- *Missiology and ethics* wrestle with life in act 5 and what it means to live as followers and witnesses of Jesus, in the obedience of faith.
- *Eschatology* looks to the "end" of the story in acts 6 and 7, with the combination of serious warning and glorious hope that pervades them, to the extent that our limited comprehension can even begin to imagine them.

Can you see how the whole Bible story shapes and informs our doctrinal construction? The whole Christian faith and all our core

Christian doctrines flow from the grand narrative of Scripture and only make sense within it and in the light of its truth. It is because *these things happened* (God's deeds and words) that *these statements of belief are true* (our creeds and doctrines).

Of course, to say that the Bible and its grand narrative should govern our systematic theology and doctrinal constructs is not to say that it always has. It is not just the case that the church has sometimes strayed far from biblical teaching in its own teachings and practice, creating the periodic need for radical recall to its scriptural roots (as in the Reformation, for example). It also happens that some doctrinal controversies arise and perpetuate themselves when doctrines are promulgated based not on close attention to the whole Bible narrative (including the Old Testament) but on concepts, questions, or analogies drawn from far distant historical eras, cultures, and worldviews, such as the Platonic dualism or the Aristotelian ontological categories of Greek philosophy, or the honor and satisfaction culture of medieval Europe.

This is perhaps nowhere more apparent than in the doctrine of the atonement, which is central to the whole biblical and Christian faith. Through the ages and today, so-called theories of the atonement have arisen and generated argument and controversy, which are sometimes brought about by models and explanations that pay scant attention to how the New Testament sets the meaning of Christ's death and resurrection within the overarching biblical narrative. And as we have seen, that governing narrative includes the covenant promises of the God of Israel; the story of Israel's election in Abraham and redemption in the exodus; Israel's failure, "death and resurrection" in exile and return; and the implications of the promised reign of God through Israel's Davidic Messiah for the blessing of all nations and all creation. That is, the New Testament writers (taking their cue from Jesus himself, as in Luke 24:44–48) repeatedly explain what God accomplished in act 4 by constant reference to God's promises and actions in act 3, not only to the fall of humanity in act 2.[10] Or, in short, we easily overlook the implications of Paul's

10. The biblical deficiency of some evangelical traditions in this area (whether in theologies of the atonement or in the practice of evangelism) is evident in the "jump" that is often made from Genesis 3 (the fall, act 2) straight to Jesus and the cross

insistence that the gospel declares that Christ died for our sins and rose again *"in accordance with the Scriptures"* (1 Cor. 15:3–4 ESV), meaning, of course, the Old Testament. Yet how many books on the atonement give no attention to those Old Testament Scriptures, other than a typological reading of the sacrificial system and the Day of Atonement.

Evangelicalism, the tradition in which I gladly stand, has been much given to creating doctrinal statements. These have often taken the form of short "statements of faith," summarizing the core beliefs that evangelicals believe to be essential to biblical, Christian faith. By their nature (as brief statements), these tend to condense doctrines into propositions using abstract nouns (like *inspiration, justification, reconciliation, sanctification, judgment,* etc.). The flavor is mostly of affirmations (or denials) to which we are expected to give cognitive assent (or not). "This is what *we believe.*" And where they quote or allude to biblical texts, these texts tend to be predominantly from the New Testament.

In 2009 I was invited to work with a group of theologians from every continent to produce a fresh statement of Christian belief in preparation for the Third Lausanne Congress on World Evangelization, which took place in Cape Town, South Africa, in 2010. The initial drafting and final editing was mine, after much consultation with the group. The outcome was the Cape Town Commitment, part 1: "For the Lord We Love: The Cape Town Confession of Faith."[11]

As I worked on this, I had three dominant intentions. First, I determined to write in a more actively narrative way, as the Bible itself mainly does, rather than simply collating abstract nouns and doctrinal concepts. Of course, there are straightforward propositional affirmations of truth that we must make, just as the Bible certainly does. But these affirmations need to be framed within the language

---

(the climax of act 4), as if nothing in act 3 (the largest part of the Bible!) is of any relevance to understanding or explaining "the gospel." It is hard to imagine Jesus or Paul explaining what they meant by "the gospel" without any reference to what we now call the Old Testament. I sometimes wonder if presentations of the gospel that leave out three quarters of the Bible can really be deemed "biblical."

11. This document can be found online at the Lausanne Movement's "Cape Town Commitment" webpage, https://lausanne.org/content/ctc/ctcommitment#capetown.

not only of "this is what *we believe*" but also of "this is what *God has done*." Wherever possible, I wanted to show how our Christian faith, especially the gospel itself, makes sense within the coherence of the whole Bible story.

And that meant, secondly, that I sought to bring Old Testament texts into the document much more than has been common in past evangelical statements. If the articulation of our faith is to be aligned with that of Jesus himself and his apostles, then surely it must be as thoroughly rooted as theirs was in what they simply called "the Scriptures." They had no problem with what we call the Old Testament! It is ironic (and grievous since it has generated so much misunderstanding) that our tendency to ask the puzzled question, Is the Old Testament really *Christian*? is actually the reverse of the question the earliest Christians, before the New Testament existed, felt they had to answer satisfactorily. *Their* question was, Is the Christian church *scriptural*? That is, can we justify our ecclesial and missional theology and practice from the authoritative (Old Testament) Scriptures? Answering that question with a clear "Yes!" was a task to which Paul gave so much space in his letters, as did the evangelists in the Gospels and Acts. So I wanted to show some areas of organic continuity between the Old and New Testaments in the framing of our faith—while, of course, making very clear the unique and climactic "new thing" that came with the incarnation and all of act 4.

Thirdly, although evangelicalism *as a movement and culture* has characteristically stressed the need for conversion, an ethically transformed life, and activism in mission, *evangelical statements of faith* have tended to list only what we believe in our heads—the cognitive, confessional dimension of faith as affirmation (or denial). Biblically, however, faith involves not just our *heads* but also our *hearts* (the commitment of the will) and our *hands* (practical good works as the proof and fruit of faith). Faith without works is dead, said James. And that threefold combination of knowledge, trusting commitment, and practical obedience is fundamentally covenantal—and fundamentally scriptural (Old Testament–related) also.

Much discussion and controversy in mission circles revolves around the question of what has priority or "primacy." Well, Jesus told us what the *first* and greatest commandment is, from Deuteronomy:

> Hear, O Israel: The Lord our God, the Lord is one. Love the Lord your God with all your heart and with all your soul and with all your strength. These commandments that I give you today are to be on your hearts. Impress them on your children. Talk about them when you sit at home and when you walk along the road, when you lie down and when you get up. Tie them as symbols on your hands and bind them on your foreheads. Write them on the doorframes of your houses and on your gates. (Deut. 6:4–9)

Can you see the heads, hearts, and hands in that foundational word? You could not get more *propositional* than the great indicative affirmation that launches it in verse 4—the oneness and uniqueness of Yahweh, the covenant God of Israel. That is the truth that Israel must *know* (note the reinforcing exhortations in Deut. 4:32–39). But it is immediately followed by the *imperative* of love, a love that implies obedience in every area of life, in the home and in the public sphere (the gate). What fills our *heads* must move our *hearts* and govern our *hands*. Faith must embrace knowing the truth about God, directing our affections and will into loving God, and living in obedience to God in daily life.

"If you love me, keep my commands," said Jesus (John 14:15; cf. vv. 21, 23)—speaking in authentic Deuteronomic terms. Paul strove for the same goal. His life's mission, he said, was to bring about *"the obedience of faith* . . . among all the nations" (Rom. 1:5 ESV; cf. 16:26), and he rejoiced when that obedience was demonstrably the outworking of love (1 Thess. 1:2–3).

Accordingly, I chose to frame every paragraph of part 1 of the Cape Town Commitment, which outlines major doctrines of our Christian faith, *in the language of covenantal love.* And in faithfulness to that Deuteronomic and Johannine dynamic, this meant stating not only what *we believe* in each case but what each belief implies for the way *we live.* I did not want a structure that separated "doctrine" from "ethics"; rather, I wanted one that showed that every so-called doctrine (i.e., teaching we understand from the

Bible) is integrally and inseparably suffused with biblical demands and motivations.

For that is how the Bible as a whole story works. It records God's self-revelation through God's actions ("what the Bible teaches") and how God has called people to respond ("how the Bible calls us to live"). Then it celebrates when those people respond well, and more often, it laments when they fail. The great story governs our doctrine *and* our ethics. That was the dynamic I tried to model in the Cape Town Commitment. I sought to allow *the Bible as a whole* to govern that one attempt, however brief and inadequate, to articulate a summary of the Christian faith, expressed as Paul would say, in "the obedience of faith." A missional hermeneutic impacts the way we do (and live out) our systematic theology.

And that brings us to a final effect, which will require more than we can fit into this chapter.

A Missional Hermeneutic Sends Us Out to Play Our Part in the Mission of God

Reading the whole Bible in this way impacts our own personal and collective sense of *purpose*. What are *we* here for, meaning we as individual Christians and as churches? For it is not merely that we are to live "in" the Bible's story; we are also summoned to live *for* the Bible's story. The goal of its story must govern the goal of our lives.

Once we understand that the Bible is a *purposeful* story, driven forward by the plan and purpose of God, then we also realize that our lives now are to be part of the way God has chosen to accomplish that plan. The whole Bible story constitutes the amazing, vast, comprehensive mission of God—which embraces all time, all nations, and all creation—in and through Christ (Eph. 1:9–10). And, amazingly, God calls us to play our part in that massive agenda.

Our mission, both as individuals and as the church, is to participate in God's mission, as "God's co-workers." This missional *story* calls for a missional *people*. What that involves will be the subject of our next chapter.

4

The Great Commission and the Five Marks of Mission

With this chapter we move from the first part of this book's title to the second, from the great story to the Great Commission. That latter term is actually of relatively recent origin within the two millennia of Christian history. It is not, of course, a term used in the Bible itself (even though it appears now as a subheading in the NIV and ESV and as a page header in the NRSV). It seems to have arisen in the early Protestant missionary era. William Carey (1761–1834) did appeal to the text of Matthew 28:18–20 as his justification for advocating foreign missions "for the conversion of the heathens,"[1] and he did speak of that passage as "the commission given by our Lord"; but he did not label it as the Great Commission. The term was popularized, however, by Hudson Taylor in the late nineteenth century, and it became a stock phrase across the whole range of missionary movements and agencies thereafter. So it is likely that any reader of this book knows by heart the words that have been labeled the Great Commission for the past century and a half.

1. William Carey, *An Enquiry into the Obligations of Christians to Use Means for the Conversion of the Heathens* (Leicester, 1792).

The Great Commission

Then Jesus came to them and said, "All authority in heaven and on earth has been given to me. Therefore go and make disciples of all nations, baptizing them in the name of the Father and of the Son and of the Holy Spirit, and teaching them to obey everything I have commanded you. And surely I am with you always, to the very end of the age." (Matt. 28:18–20)

Now the first thing we should note about this text, after all we have seen in the previous chapters, is how remarkably well it tracks with the great biblical narrative. It begins with creation, since "heaven and earth" was the standard Jewish way of referring to all creation (as in Gen. 1:1 and Rev. 21:1, as well as in Pauline passages such as Eph. 1:10 and Col. 1:15–20). So acts 1 and 2 are there, since the authority Jesus has over all creation includes his definitive triumph over all the tragic impacts of the fall. There are strong echoes of Deuteronomy, as we shall see, in language that recalls God's words to Israel in act 3. The gospel offer of entering into relationship with God as Father, Son, and Holy Spirit is founded on Christ's revelatory teaching and atoning accomplishment in act 4. The task of making disciples of all nations, and the promised presence of Jesus as we do so, is the substance of act 5. And that concluding promise looks forward to "the very end of the age"—which brings us to acts 6 and 7.

The whole Bible is implied in the Great Commission! It is a truly comprehensive statement and a colossal vista with which Matthew ends his Gospel. Having acknowledged what a spectacularly rich and programmatic text it is, however, let me inject two caveats.

First of all, we are not arguing in this chapter that the Great Commission is the only or the most important biblical text on which our theology and practice of mission can or should be built. But it has become the dominant one in many quarters, by the very label that has been attached to it (i.e., *the* Great Commission), by the categorizing use of that label,[2] and by exclusive emphasis on one or another short

2. Like the many "Great Commission Churches" and "Great Commission Christians" that appear as statistical categories in some surveys of world Christianity.

phrase within the whole text.[3] However, as anyone will know who is at all familiar with my work in *The Mission of God* and *The Mission of God's People* (or has at least absorbed the last three chapters of this book), I am convinced that we need the whole Bible for a full understanding of what we mean by the word *mission* (just as we need the whole Bible to understand the "whole counsel of God" or indeed the "whole gospel of God").

Or to be more precise (and of far greater significance), we need the Old Testament Scriptures for a full understanding of whatever we think *Jesus meant* his disciples to be and go and do. For Luke tells us very clearly (in his version of Christ's final commission to his disciples in Luke 24:44–49) that Jesus opened their minds to every part of the canon of Scripture (i.e., the Law, the Prophets, and the Writings—the three great sections of what we now call the Old Testament), not only to explain what had just happened to *him*, but also to program the task that now awaited *them*. The mission of the church (if we want to use that phrase to describe what Jesus meant by "You are witnesses of these things"; Luke 24:48) is founded on his assertion that *"this is what is written"* (Luke 24:46)—that is, on the whole message of Scripture, not just a single text at the end of one Gospel.

Nevertheless, having made that point, and for the sake of those who do place the fullest weight of their theology of mission on that glorious text at the end of Matthew, I hope to show how a biblically comprehensive and integrated understanding of mission can be carefully and theologically linked to the full meaning of the Great Commission and its scripturally pregnant phrases.

The second caveat is that when we observe how thoroughly *God*-centered and *Christ*-centered the Great Commission is, it should restrain our tendency to shift its focus entirely onto *us* and *our* missional aspirations, agendas, urgencies, and timetables. The text is obviously Christ-centered, since it is Christ who is speaking and his words begin with the affirmation of his lordship and end with the promise of his presence. But it is also God-centered inasmuch as (1) the opening affirmation explicitly echoes what is said about

3. I well remember the slogan on the walls and platform of a great missionary convention I spoke at some years ago: "Just go!" it exhorted. I remember thinking, "Just hold on! That's not what Jesus actually said."

Yahweh, the God of Israel (e.g., in Deut. 4:39), and (2) the closing promise echoes one of the most prominent and precious promises that Yahweh makes to his servants and his people in the Old Testament—"I am with you." Jesus is speaking as none other than the Lord God of Israel, incarnate, crucified, and risen.

Furthermore, given that this is the way Matthew chooses to end his Gospel, we can sense an echo of Jesus's words to Peter at that pivotal revelatory moment at Caesarea Philippi. "I will build my church," says Jesus, "and the gates of Hades will not overcome it" (Matt. 16:18). In these final words, it is as if Jesus is saying, "Yes, *I will indeed* build my church, and here's how I will do it: *you* will go and make disciples of all nations, baptizing them into relationship with the Father, Son, and Holy Spirit, and teaching them so that they become a community of faithful obedience to me, true followers who obey all I commanded you."

In other words, this is as much an ecclesial manifesto by the Lord of the church (what he intends to do) as it is a missional agenda for members of the church (what they must go and do). In fact, it is integrally and simultaneously both.

So surely we diminish these great christological and theocentric contours of the text when it is portrayed mainly as a project *we* have to somehow manage and achieve[4]—or, worse, as a kind of ticking clock with a timetable that can only be "fulfilled" when *we* complete the task. As if the Lord who is building his church is waiting for us to "finish the job" for him before he can return. This is not, of course, to diminish (conversely) the unquestionably imperatival and mandatory nature of Christ's words. *There is* a task entrusted to us here, to which all disciples are summoned and committed. The problem arises if we imagine God as somehow dependent on our response or inactive in the world apart from it.

I question this whole use (abuse?) of the Great Commission in *The Mission of God*:

> What happens if one questions the common assumption that this text gives some kind of timetable for the return of Christ: he will come

_____

4. "What will it take to get the job done?" is how I have heard it put in conferences on world evangelization.

back just as soon as we have all the nations discipled? And is discipling a task that can ever be said to be completed (noting in passing that the text does say "disciple," not evangelize)? *Doesn't every fresh generation of long-evangelized nations need fresh discipling?* The Great Commission is an expanding and self-replicating task, not a ticking clock for the end times.[5]

Whose Mission Is It?

This tendency to see the Great Commission, and mission in general, as primarily *ours* seems to be one reason there is so much disagreement around the word *mission* itself. We argue over what mission actually is, about right and wrong ways of doing it, about what is "real mission" and "not real mission," and even whether we should still be using the word at all, as we touched on in the introduction to this book. I have been known to enter such arguments myself.[6]

Sometimes the cause of so much disagreement is that we tend to have a very human-centered concept of mission, illustrated in the way we translate the Great Commission merely into a management project for ourselves. This anthropocentrism appears whether we are thinking of those who are the hoped-for beneficiaries of mission (sinners in need of salvation) or of those who are the hopeful agents of mission (saints in need of a purpose). We go around the same endless arguments over relative human needs and priorities. Even some of the popular buzzwords don't settle the arguments.

Holistic mission, for example, implies that mission should respond to whole people in their spiritual, material, social, and environmental existence and needs. Agreed. But then, what do people need most? Shouldn't we prioritize their greatest need, presumably the spiritual dimension? But is God only interested in "souls"? The argument goes back and forth endlessly.

---

5. Christopher J. H. Wright, *The Mission of God: Unlocking the Bible's Grand Narrative* (Downers Grove, IL: IVP Academic, 2006), 35 (italics added). See also a recent "friendly critique" in Stefan Paas, *Pilgrims and Priests: Christian Mission in Post-Christian Society* (London: SCM, 2019), 68–74.

6. See, e.g., Jason S. Sexton, ed., *Four Views on the Church's Mission*, Counterpoints: Bible and Theology (Grand Rapids: Zondervan, 2017).

Missional church has become a popular label and claim. But, then again, what should a "missional church" be doing that is really missional? Is *everything* a church does counted as mission? Doesn't that dilute the whole concept? Aren't some things more "missional" than others? And so the arguments slew round and round amid competing taxonomies of human needs and church priorities. And the depressing result is that we end up separating what, in my biblical understanding, God has joined together.

But, as I've been trying to stress, our proper starting point in thinking about mission *biblically* should be first of all *the mission of God*, the divine, sovereign purpose that is the governing theme of the whole Bible narrative. What does the Bible tell us about the overarching plan and purpose of God for the whole creation and the human race? Only when we have gotten hold of that should we go on to ask (as we must) the follow-up question: What is the mission of God's people, as we participate in the mission of God himself? Who are we and what are we here for?

One of the most concise answers to that first question is given by Paul in Ephesians 1:9–10: "[God] made known to us the mystery of his will according to his good pleasure, which he purposed in Christ, to be put into effect when the times reach their fulfillment—to bring unity to all things in heaven and on earth under Christ."

Now, as I pointed out in chapter 3, when Paul speaks of God's "will" here and in the closely related text of Colossians 1:9, he does not mean God's personal guidance for our individual lives but God's great cosmic purpose throughout all time and space. That is probably what Paul meant by "the whole counsel of God" (Acts 20:27 ESV). It is the plan of God from Genesis to Revelation, centered on and held together by Christ. Paul is saying that the mission of God is to bring healing, reconciliation, and unity to the whole creation in and through Christ. That is God's great agenda for the cosmos and for the whole of human history on this planet. It lifts us beyond what we can imagine, and it puts all our missional efforts into proper Christocentric perspective, within the sovereignty God.

So when the Cape Town Commitment comes to define the mission to which we are committed, it very quickly shifts gears into

summarizing the mission of God himself. As you read this paragraph,
notice the echoes of Scripture, including Genesis and Revelation.

> We are committed to world mission, because it is central to our
> understanding of God, the Bible, the Church, human history and the
> ultimate future. The whole Bible reveals the mission of God to bring
> all things in heaven and earth into unity under Christ, reconciling
> them through the blood of his cross. In fulfilling his mission, God will
> transform the creation broken by sin and evil into the new creation
> in which there is no more sin or curse. God will fulfil his promise
> to Abraham to bless all nations on the earth, through the gospel of
> Jesus, the Messiah, the seed of Abraham. God will transform the
> fractured world of nations that are scattered under the judgment of
> God into the new humanity that will be redeemed by the blood of
> Christ from every tribe, nation, people and language, and will be
> gathered to worship our God and Saviour. God will destroy the reign
> of death, corruption and violence when Christ returns to establish
> his eternal reign of life, justice and peace. Then God, Immanuel,
> will dwell with us, and the kingdom of the world will become the
> kingdom of our Lord and of his Christ and he shall reign for ever
> and ever.[7]

Amen! That great vista should fill us with worship and thanksgiving. Praise God for the great mission that *God himself* will assuredly accomplish! But we are still left wondering, So what? What
about *us*? Who are *we*, as God's people, and what are we here for?
What is *our* mission?

Well, at least that full biblical sweep of the mission of God
should prepare us to expect a comparably broad answer to those
questions. *Our* mission, surely, must be to participate with God in
God's mission—to be, as Paul said, "God's fellow workers," "working together with him" (1 Cor. 3:9; 2 Cor. 6:1 ESV). And that means
that God calls us into a very far-reaching and wide-ranging agenda
indeed. This does not mean, of course, that we can (or should even
try to) "do all that God does." That would be an absurd arrogance;

---

7. Third Lausanne Congress, "The Cape Town Commitment: A Confession of
Faith and a Call to Action" (Lausanne Movement, 2011), 1.10, https://lausanne.org
/content/ctc/ctcommitment#capetown.

God is sovereign and active far beyond the bounds of our obedience (or otherwise). But it does mean that what we do in obedience to the Lord Jesus Christ must reflect and respond in some way to the range of what God himself plans and wills to be done through his people.

With that in mind, let's move on to think about how we might define the mission of the church.[8]

The Five Marks of Mission

There have been many proposals over many years, of course, to define and describe the mission of the church. One that I find helpful was produced by the Anglican Consultative Council in 1984. It was conceived as a mission statement for the worldwide Anglican Communion and was adopted by the Lambeth Conference of bishops in 1988 as the "Five Marks of Mission." I am not suggesting it is the only or the best summary of key components of Christian mission, but it has proved valuable, and some churches (including my own home church, All Souls Church, Langham Place, London) use it for a kind of "mission audit"—to check whether, as a community of believers, we are involved, in some way at least, in all five areas of missional engagement, sending, support, prayer, and funding. The "five marks" scheme has also generated some further exploratory literature.[9]

8. The following section refers primarily to the mission of the Christian church in the post-Pentecost era. However, as we seek to unpack what that is, we cannot avoid using the Old Testament. For, while the church as the multinational community of those who are united by explicit faith in Jesus of Nazareth may be regarded as birthed at Pentecost, the people of God go back in spiritual continuity to Abraham. And so, in order to articulate what kind of people God has chosen and called to serve his mission in the world, we need to pay detailed attention to what God required of Israel. This is especially needed since so much that Jesus and the apostles insist on for the life and witness of the church is deeply rooted in the Scriptures of the Holy One of Israel, as we shall see below. I have explored the breadth of the Old Testament's answer to the question, What kind of people does God want for his mission? in *The Mission of God's People: A Biblical Theology of the Church's Mission*, Biblical Theology for Life (Grand Rapids: Zondervan, 2010).

9. See, e.g., Andrew Walls and Cathy Ross, eds., *Mission in the Twenty-First Century: Exploring the Five Marks of Mission* (Maryknoll, NY: Orbis Books, 2008).

The statement affirms that

The mission of the church is the mission of Christ

1. To proclaim the Good News of the Kingdom
2. To teach, baptise and nurture new believers
3. To respond to human need by loving service
4. To transform unjust structures of society, to challenge violence of every kind and pursue peace and reconciliation
5. To strive to safeguard the integrity of creation, and sustain and renew the life of the earth[10]

These could be summarized in a few words: *evangelism, teaching, compassion, justice,* and *responsible use and care of creation.* It is a remarkably comprehensive and holistic list, and each of the five items can be shown to have deep roots in the Bible. As we look at each of them in the following chapters, I would emphasize two things as crucial presuppositions in each case: (1) these five marks are rooted in what God himself is doing in the world (our mission shares in God's mission), and (2) all five marks can be related to dimensions of the Great Commission. Let's consider each of these.

First, all of the five marks can be considered as ways in which we do actually participate in the mission of God. When *we* do these things, *God* is actively at work with us and we with him. That is because all these things are clearly identified in the Bible as passionate

10. "Marks of Mission," Anglican Communion, Anglican Communion Office, accessed January 28, 2022, https://www.anglicancommunion.org/mission/marks-of -mission.aspx. Since 1984 there has been ongoing debate around the "five marks" and some modification of the terminology. But the essential thrust of them remains, even under different expressions. For example, the Anglican Board of Mission in Australia recently reframed them as follows:

1. Witness to Christ's saving, forgiving, reconciling love for all people.
2. Build welcoming, transforming communities of faith.
3. Stand in solidarity with the poor and needy.
4. Challenge violence, injustice and oppression, and work for peace and reconciliation.
5. Protect, care for and renew life on our planet.

"ABM Welcomes Change to the Marks of Mission," Anglican Communion News Service, Anglican Communion Office, January 24, 2013, http://www.anglicannews .org/news/2013/01/abm-welcomes-change-to-the-marks-of-mission.aspx.

concerns of God. All of them are true of God. If these are marks of *our* mission, it is because they flow from the character, actions, and mission of God.

1. God is the evangelist, the origin of the good news, as the One who promised, achieved, and proclaimed it.
2. God is our teacher, Christ being the head from whom we grow into maturity.
3. God self-identifies in the Old Testament as the compassionate, gracious, and loving God.
4. The same Scriptures affirm that justice is the foundation of God's throne.
5. God rules over, loves, and provides and cares for his whole creation.

Each of those affirmations could be corroborated with abundant and explicit biblical support.

So, when a church that is reflecting on and planning its own mission theology, strategy, and practice (in the conviction that all churches *should* do so) is informed and intentional in these five areas, that church is actively participating with God and his mission. Such a church can legitimately see all their efforts as flowing from and fruitful within that prior mission of God. God is already at work in all these ways, and we are co-workers with him.

Our mandate, then, is not so much to "get the job done *for God*" but to "join *with God* in the work of God's mission." This carefully nuanced perspective does two things. On the one hand, it generates *humility*: *we* are not the superheroes of mission who are going to save the world. Let God be God. But thankfully, on the other hand, it generates *hope* because it guarantees ultimate *success*: for whatever the inadequacies and struggles and limited time frame of all our missional efforts, God is at work and will be faithful to his own promises and eschatological goal. God wins! The mission is God's; humility and hope are ours.

Secondly, I also believe that all five marks of mission can be linked (directly or indirectly) to the Great Commission. I say this, to repeat,

not because that is the only or most important missional text in the
Bible, but rather for the sake of those who tend to give it a very high
level of mandatory and motivational weight (as I do myself). I hope
to help us all see that *the Great Commission itself* embraces a greater,
holistic comprehensiveness than we may have so far imagined.

All five marks can be integrated around the Great Commission,
provided (and this is a very big *provided*) we put at the center of all of
them Christ's great opening affirmation—the lordship of Christ over
all creation. This is utterly essential. All five dimensions of mission
depend on the lordship of Christ. That is why, in figure 4.1, I have
linked them all together around the centrality of that cosmic truth.

- In evangelism we proclaim the good news that Jesus Christ is
  Lord, King, and Savior.
- In teaching and discipling, we bring people into maturity of
  faith and understanding and ever deepening submission to
  Jesus Christ as Lord.
- In works of loving compassion, we follow the example of
  the Lord Jesus, who, embodying the character of the Lord
  God of Israel (Exod. 34:6–8), "went about doing good" (Acts
  10:38 ESV), in acts of sometimes-scandalous kindness.
- In seeking justice we remember that the crucified and risen
  Lord Jesus Christ is at the center of God's throne (Rev. 5:6)
  and that "righteousness and justice are the foundation of
  [God's] throne" (Ps. 97:2).
- In ruling, using, and caring for God's creation, we are han-
  dling what belongs to the Lord Jesus Christ (1 Cor. 10:26),
  by right of creation, redemption, and inheritance (Col.
  1:15–20).

We do all these things as distinct but integrated dimensions of our
missional intentionality and action entirely *because* Jesus is Lord
of heaven and earth. It is *his* eternal and universal authority that
provides sufficient temporal and earthly authority for *our action*.

Figure 4.1 shows those five marks, then, joined to one another,
integrated, and held together by the centrality of the gospel truth

Fig. 4.1. The Five Marks of Mission

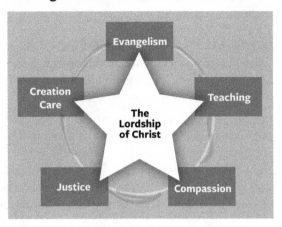

that Jesus is Lord. The lordship of Christ is another way (Paul's main way) of expressing the kingdom of God, since the reign of God was announced, embodied, and inaugurated by Jesus. To proclaim "Jesus is Lord" is tantamount to proclaiming with Israel's psalmists, "The LORD [Yahweh] reigns." And that proclaimed fact, as the psalmists celebrated in advance, is the gospel, *the good news* that must be announced among all nations to the ends of the earth (see Pss. 96–99 especially).[11]

Three Focal Points of Mission

While each of the five marks has its own distinct domain, I think we can simplify our diagram by grouping four of them into two pairs (see fig. 4.2). Evangelism and teaching belong together. Similarly, compassion and justice are closely related. This then creates *three* major missional tasks, or three focal points for our missional

11. On the centrality of the kingdom of God in the life and teaching of Jesus and its consequent centrality in a biblical understanding of the gospel and the mission of the church, see Ed Stetzer, "An Evangelical Kingdom Community Approach," in *The Mission of the Church: Five Views in Conversation,* ed. Craig Ott (Grand Rapids: Baker Academic, 2016), 91–116; and Scot McKnight, *Kingdom Conspiracy: Returning to the Radical Mission of the Local Church* (Grand Rapids: Brazos, 2016).

engagement: *church*, *society*, and *creation*. Mission, on this viewing, involves

1. *building the church*[12] through evangelism and teaching; bringing individual sinners to repentance, faith, baptism, and obedience as disciples of Jesus Christ; and building them up to maturity in the fellowship of God's holy people;

2. *serving society*[13] through active works of compassion and justice-seeking (which includes reconciliation and peacemaking); responding to Jesus sending us into the world to be salt and light (Matt. 5:13–16); being doers of good, created for and committed to "good works" (meaning public good), as Paul insisted (Eph. 2:10; Titus 2:14; 3:1, 8, 14); and seeking the

---

12. Some might object to this phrase on the grounds that *we* don't "build the church," which is Christ's own work. The same accusation might arise if I said "growing the church," for it is God who makes things grow. Nevertheless, we avoid any sense of arrogance when we remember the astonishing *cooperative* nature of what God does *along with* or *through* human means. Who brought the Israelites out of Egypt? God, obviously. Yet at the very point when God announces "*I* have come down . . . to bring them up out of that land," he says to Moses, "So now, go. I am sending *you* . . . to bring my people the Israelites out of Egypt" (Exod. 3:8–10). Paul knew that building the church was Christ's work, but he could still talk about himself laying a foundation as a wise builder and about others building on it (1 Cor. 3:10). And, as I suggested above, the Great Commission itself can be read as if Jesus were saying, "I, the Lord of heaven and earth, will build my church, and here's how: you go and make disciples, and I will be with you, as I was with Moses."

13. I deliberately chose the word *serving* here and throughout the following chapters, rather than *changing* or *transforming*. I do strongly believe, as will be evident, that communities of faithful Christian witness and action have the capacity, under God, to make a difference in their environments—social, economic, environmental, and so on. That surely is implied in being "salt and light" in the world. But ambitions or claims to "transform the world" as a goal of *our* mission (as distinct from the eschatological goal of God's mission) can become hubristic and doomed to disillusionment. I take heed here of the critique of such thinking by Paas, *Pilgrims and Priests*, 74–86. This is not, however, to criticize earlier use of the language of "transformation" to refer to the nature and impact of gospel-centered holistic mission, or integral mission, to use the more recent terminology. See the fine explanation, survey, and bibliography provided by Ruth Padilla DeBorst in "An Integral Transformation Approach: Being, Doing and Saying," in Ott, *The Mission of the Church*, 41–67, and the work of INFEMIT, the International Fellowship for Mission as Transformation, https://infemit.org.

welfare of the people around us, as Jeremiah told the Israelites in Babylon (Jer. 29:7 ESV); and

3. *caring for creation* through wise economic use of the resources of creation in all our daily work, along with ecological concern and action, fulfilling the very first "great commission" that God gave to humanity in Genesis 1 and 2.

You'll notice that I have kept that primary affirmation central: "All authority in heaven and on earth has been given to me." Everything we do in mission, everything related to all three of these domains, flows from the cosmic lordship of Jesus Christ.

- We build the *church* because Jesus is Lord of the church, the community of saved and reconciled sinners.
- We serve *society* because Jesus (not "Caesar" or any of his successors) is Lord of every nation, government, and culture (whether acknowledged as such or not). He is "the ruler of the kings of the earth" (Rev. 1:5). We serve society, of course,

Fig. 4.2. Church, Society, Creation

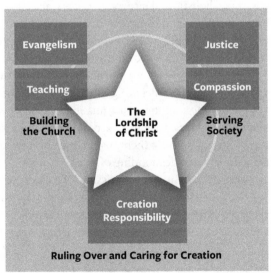

wherever possible under the legitimate authority of human governments, but we do so under the ultimate authority of the Lord Christ, King Jesus.

- We care for *creation* because Jesus is Lord of heaven *and earth*. "The earth is the LORD's, and everything in it" (Ps. 24:1). Paul quotes this verse, in which the psalmist refers to Yahweh, but in Paul's context "the Lord" clearly means Jesus (1 Cor. 10:26; this is greatly amplified in Col. 1:15–23).

Every dimension of our mission, then, flows from the lordship of Christ and from God's invincible intention that the whole world and all creation will come to recognize that Jesus is Lord—and in doing so, will come to know, love, praise, and worship our creator and redeemer God. Keeping the lordship of Christ at the center enables us to integrate (hold together) all our missional engagement around the centrality of the gospel—the good news as proclaimed by Jesus himself (that God in Christ is King) and by Paul (that God was in Christ reconciling the world to himself).

As with the five marks of mission that are built into it, I believe this triple focus and scope of mission (church, society, and creation) is fully biblical. The Cape Town Commitment recognizes a similar *triple focus* within a holistic and integrated understanding of mission: "Integral mission means discerning, proclaiming, and living out, the biblical truth that the gospel is God's good news, through the cross and resurrection of Jesus Christ, for individual persons, *and* for society, *and* for creation. All three are broken and suffering because of sin; all three are included in the redeeming love and mission of God; all three must be part of the comprehensive mission of God's people."[14]

In the following chapters, we will go around those three main focal points of our diagram, holding them together around the centrality of the gospel within our understanding of integral mission and seeing how they connect to the Great Commission. We shall consider the first, building the church, in chapter 5; then serving society in chapter 6; and then we will turn to creation in chapters 7 and 8.

---

14. Third Lausanne Congress, "The Cape Town Commitment," 1.7a (italics original), https://lausanne.org/content/ctc/ctcommitment#p1-7.

5

Building the Church through Evangelism and Teaching

"Make disciples," said Jesus, "baptizing them . . . *and* teaching them . . ."

Baptizing new believers must, of course, presuppose the task of evangelism, our first "mark of mission." This follows as the first and most obvious implication of what Jesus had just announced. For if Jesus of Nazareth is truly Lord of all creation (as indeed he is), and if he addresses us as the Lord God of Israel, Maker of heaven and earth (as he does), then we who are addressed by him are summoned first of all, like Israel of old, to submit to his lordship in grateful trust and obedience—*to become and to be his disciples* within the realm of the kingdom of God that he announced and inaugurated. And then, at his command, we are *to make disciples* by inviting others to hear the good news about Jesus and what God has accomplished in him and to respond in the same way that he called for in his earthly ministry—in repentance, faith, and obedience.

Evangelism

It is a pity that the words *gospel* and *evangelism* have separated in the English language, since they are in the same word group in Greek.

And the Greek word *euangelion* (good news or gospel; *evangelium* in Latin) was not originally a Christian word at all. It was a street word common enough in the Roman Empire (often in the plural form *euangelia*—like our "news" for "new things") for a public announcement of some event that had taken place and was claimed to be good news for everybody. It would be proclaimed, for example, when a battle was won (good news, of course, provided you supported the winner) or a new emperor came to power, or in the wake of some great imperial accomplishment (real or alleged), like bringing peace to the whole world (as Augustus Caesar claimed).

Also, the word (as a verb, to announce good news) was already used by those who translated the Hebrew Scriptures of the Old Testament into Greek in the centuries before Christ. When the psalmist wants Yahweh's name and salvation to be proclaimed as good news among the nations, this is the Greek word (*euangelizomai*) that the translators chose for the Hebrew verb *basar*, which meant "to bring good news" (see, e.g., Ps. 96:1–3). It's the same word used when Isaiah pictures the messenger running to bring to Jerusalem the good news that the exile is ending and God the Redeemer is returning with his people (Isa. 52:7).

So when Mark begins his "Gospel" with the word *euangelion*— "the beginning of *the good news* about Jesus the Messiah, the Son of God" (Mark 1:1)—he can tap into a word that both resonated (for Jews) with good news about the God of Israel and also was familiar to gentiles who only ever heard "good news" as some glossy propaganda of the Roman Empire.

For the apostles had a *euangelion* to proclaim that far surpassed any announcement by the Roman Empire. Their good news was not about some claimed achievement by a mere Caesar. Theirs was good news about something the one, true, living God had done in the course of eye-witnessed public events in real history. It is important to realize that the word we translate as "gospel" has this primary meaning: the announcing, as good news, of *something that has already happened*, actual events that you need to know about, events that are for your benefit if you respond rightly to the announcement.

So *evangelism* simply means "gospeling" the good news of what God has promised and accomplished through Christ. We need to avoid using the word *gospel* as a formula for getting to heaven, or as shorthand for "the sinner's prayer," or merely as a concept that we are asked to believe in our heads (or as a handy emoji kind of adjective to attach to a person or an activity or a church that we happen to approve of).

It is so easy for the anthropocentrism that we saw in relation to *mission* to creep into our way of thinking and talking about the *gospel* itself. We use the word as if it is all about us, when in fact it is first of all good news *about God and what God has done*. That's why Paul can speak of it categorically as "the gospel of God" (Rom. 1:1), which seems to combine the senses of "good news *from* God" and "good news *about* God." Either way, it is *God's* good news! That is what makes it such good news for us, when we hear it as something *God* has done that we *receive* with thanks, joy, faith, and love. And, of course, it is good news primarily about what God has accomplished in the historical events surrounding Jesus of Nazareth. As the Cape Town Commitment puts it,

> *We love the story the gospel tells.* The gospel announces as good news the historical events of the life, death and resurrection of Jesus of Nazareth. As the son of David, the promised Messiah King, Jesus is the one through whom alone God established his kingdom and acted for the salvation of the world, enabling all nations on earth to be blessed, as he promised Abraham. Paul defines the gospel in stating that 'Christ died for our sins according to the scriptures, that he was buried, that he was raised on the third day, according the scriptures, and that he appeared to Peter and then to the Twelve.' The gospel declares that, on the cross of Christ, God took upon himself, in the person of his Son and in our place, the judgment our sin deserves. In the same great saving act, completed, vindicated and declared through the resurrection, God won the decisive victory over Satan, death and all evil powers, liberated us from their power and fear, and ensured their eventual destruction. God accomplished the reconciliation of believers with himself and with one another across all boundaries and enmities. God also accomplished his purpose of the ultimate reconciliation of all creation, and in the bodily resurrection of Jesus has given us the first fruits of the new creation. 'God was in Christ reconciling the world to himself.' How we love the gospel story![1]

1. Third Lausanne Congress, "The Cape Town Commitment: A Confession of Faith and a Call to Action" (Lausanne Movement, 2011), 1.8b, https://lausanne.org

Evangelism, then, means telling the whole story of *what God has done* (using the Old and New Testaments). It is announcing the good news that the God who *created* the world has acted to *save* the world from the consequences of human sin and satanic evil; that God has done this through his Son, Jesus of Nazareth, who came in fulfillment of God's promise to Israel and who, as God's appointed Messiah, died for our sins and was raised to life by the power of God; that this same Jesus is now the ascended Lord who will return as Judge and King to claim his inheritance with redeemed humanity in the new creation. Evangelism is a fundamental dimension of *our* mission because, like everything else we do in obedience to Christ, it flows from and bears witness to the good news that is grounded in *God's* mission. This is what *we do* because this is what *God has done*.

Evangelism goes on to invite people to *respond* to this announcement of good news of what God has done through Christ, by turning in repentance from whatever false story they are living in and by putting their faith in Jesus for salvation. And when they do so, we can assure them in God's name that they now have a part to play in that great biblical story of God's planned future for the world, that their sin is forgiven, and that they can enjoy a right relationship with God and the gift of eternal life now and forever.

That new relationship with God is what baptism speaks of. The phrase "baptizing them *into* the name of . . ." means that all who choose to accept the good news, repent, believe, and join the community of disciples of the Lord Jesus Christ are to be baptized *into* relationship with God the Father, who loves them; God the Son, who died for them; and God the Holy Spirit, who will dwell within them and bear his fruit in their lives as they are being transformed into the likeness of Christ.

Baptism, then, is the entry point into the church of God and the defining marker of those who are deemed to belong in that "new humanity" created through the cross of Christ. Theologically, it signifies identification with Christ in his death and resurrection (e.g., Col. 2:11–12); ecclesially, it signals accepting a new identity as a child

---

/content/ctc/ctcommitment#capetown. The document lists the following references: Mark 1:1, 14–15; Rom. 1:1–4; 4:1–25; 1 Cor. 15:3–5; 1 Pet. 2:24; Col. 2:15; Heb. 2:14–15; Eph. 2:14–18; Col. 1:20; 2 Cor. 5:19.

of God and being accepted into membership in the body of Christ. It is notable in the book of Acts that the baptism of new believers regularly and *immediately* follows their confession of faith, such that it could be appealed to as the basis of the new life that must then be lived in the liberating power and fruit of the Spirit (Rom. 6:3–4; Gal. 3:26–29).

It could be said, then, if we wanted to be strictly accurate to the Great Commission, that *baptism*, as the first tool of disciple-making mentioned by Jesus, ought to be our "first mark of mission." And it is indeed regrettable not only that baptism is often neglected in many theologies and practices of mission[2] but also, more tragically, that baptism—which ought to be a foundational marker of the church's *unity* as God's new humanity in Christ—has itself become one of the most vitriolic causes of *disunity* in church history. However, inasmuch as baptism does presuppose the work of evangelism—sharing the good news and inviting people to respond to Christ—it seems appropriate to keep evangelism (including the proper and commanded response of baptism) as the first of our five marks of mission. It flows inevitably from the lordship of Christ and proclaims what Christ's lordship entails.

This immediately shows how wrong it has been in some quarters to use the phrase *holistic mission* to refer to all the other things Christians do *apart from evangelism*—such as medical and educational services, social action, development and poverty relief, advocacy and action for justice, creation care, and so on.[3] By definition, social action without evangelism is no more "holistic" than evangelism without social action. That basic understanding has been agreed on since

---

2. I have to confess my own earlier neglect in this regard. This was pointed out, quite justifiably, in Peter Leithart, "Sacramental Mission: Ecumenical and Political Missiology," in *Four Views on the Church's Mission*, ed. Jason S. Sexton, Counterpoints: Bible and Theology (Grand Rapids: Zondervan, 2017), 152–76. See particularly his observations in the section "The Forgotten Sacraments" (153–56), which include reference to this gap in my earlier books on mission. I gladly accept the rebuke.

3. I was surprised, for example, to participate in a Lausanne conference in 2004 where "Holistic Mission" labeled one of some thirty "special interest" groups and referred to social action of various kinds. I protested that "holistic" was supposed to mean "the whole thing"—not one category among others. Lausanne has since avoided that kind of labeling.

the first Lausanne Congress in 1974 and the subsequent theological clarifications that were hammered out in the following decade.[4] The more recent term *integral mission* seeks to avoid this dichotomy by stressing that everything we do in mission, *including evangelism*, must be integrated around the centrality of the gospel, the gospel of God.[5]

That is why I now prefer to speak of the "centrality of the gospel" rather than "the primacy of evangelism." Many evangelicals have pressed that latter phrase because, they argue, evangelism addresses our greatest human need. And I do not disagree with that (though it easily slides from "greatest" to "the only one that really matters" or "the only one that God really cares about"). But notice how, when we talk that way, we have slipped again into an anthropocentric concept of mission: evangelism is about what *we* do because of what *they* need. The gospel, though, is about what *God* has done. The gospel, as the New Testament uses the term, is the essential good news of the objective historical events through which *God has acted* to save the world, and evangelism is the telling of *that* story, God's story. It is the gospel itself, not our evangelism, that is the power of God unto salvation.

We may do a whole lot of things, quite legitimately, in the breadth of many missional callings (as the other "marks of mission" allude to), but the integrating heart and center of them all must be the God-centered, God-generated, and God-willed reality of the gospel. And that is nothing less than the *cosmic* story of God's redemptive purpose

4. I have attempted a summary, with bibliography, of some of the key theological developments within the Lausanne Movement in the decades after 1974, in John Stott and Christopher J. H. Wright, *Christian Mission in the Modern World*, 2nd ed. (Downers Grove, IL: IVP Books, 2015), 34–57.

5. Kirsteen Kim argues for a recovery of the longer term "evangelization," in order to embrace both the verbal and social dimensions of gospel-centered mission. "'Evangelization,' properly understood, encompasses the whole work of bringing the good news of the kingdom of God. In other words, it is a synonym for 'mission.' However, it particularly draws attention—in a way that 'mission' alone does not—to the distinctive heart of Christian mission as following in the way of Jesus Christ. His preaching of the good news was transformative both intellectually and holistically, both personally and also of families, communities, societies, and even the whole creation. Mission as evangelization is both a witness, which makes known this person and event, and at the same time a continuation of the work of Christ in the same Holy Spirit." See "Mission as Evangelization," in *Evangelism and Diakonia in Context*, ed. Rose Dowsett et al., Regnum Edinburgh Centenary Series 32 (Oxford: Regnum, 2015), 81–96.

for his whole creation, *promised* in the Old Testament, *accomplished* by the death and resurrection of Jesus Christ, *embodied* in the good news of the kingdom of God in the lordship of Christ, and to be *consummated* at his return in glory. In evangelism we tell this story. And from this story, and this story alone, all our mission flows. It is because the gospel is what it is (the historical facts) that there is a nonnegotiable imperative for us to make it known by sharing the good news in every way possible. Evangelism, I am saying, is not the only constituent element of a fully biblical mission, but no theology or practice of mission can claim to be fully biblical if it is not rooted in and governed by the biblical good news of God in Christ reconciling the world to himself and motivated and equipped to share it.

Now, when I speak of the centrality of the gospel, I do not mean a center that makes everything else peripheral—marginal and unimportant, out there, far off from the center, of secondary importance only (as the term *primacy* can seem to imply). Rather, I mean a center that *holds everything else together.*

The gospel is central in the way that a hub is central to a wheel. A wheel is an integrated, functioning object with a rim and a tire that is in contact with the road. But the full circle of the rim must be connected all the way round to the hub. In that sense *the hub is the integrating center* of all that a wheel is and does. And the hub is connected to the engine, transmitting its power to "where the rubber hits the road." To drive a car, you need integration between the hub, which is connected to the engine (the power source), and the tire, which is in contact with the road (the context). There is no point asking which is more important or has greater priority—hub or tire. Unless you have both, you haven't got a car that will drive! To engage in integral mission, you need integration between, on the one hand, the verbal sharing of the good news of the historical facts and truth of the gospel in evangelism and, on the other hand, the embodiment of that gospeling in social and contextual engagement with society and creation.

Once again, the Cape Town Commitment seeks to capture this integrated understanding of mission:

> The *source* of all our mission is what God has done in Christ for the redemption of the whole world, as revealed in the Bible. Our evangelistic

task is to make that good news known to all nations. The *context* of all our mission is the world in which we live, the world of sin, suffering, injustice, and creational disorder, into which God sends us to love and serve for Christ's sake. All our mission must therefore reflect the integration of evangelism and committed engagement in the world, both being ordered and driven by the whole biblical revelation of the gospel of God.[6]

That brings us to our second mark of mission, which is also an essential part of building the church.

Teaching and Discipling

Jesus's primary command is to "make disciples." How? His first means is "baptizing them" (presupposing the work of evangelism), and his second quickly follows: "*and teaching them* to observe all that I have commanded you" (Matt. 28:19–20 ESV). In other words, Jesus tells his disciples to make disciples in the way Jesus himself had discipled them. It's no good just bringing people to conversion and leaving it at that. The seed needs deep soil and good roots in order to bear fruit. Churches need to be not only planted through evangelism but also watered through teaching. Both evangelism *and* teaching are Great Commission mandates.

In line with what we said in the previous chapter, when we engage in teaching as a component of *our* mission, we are also sharing in a component of the mission of *God*. For *God himself* is at work not only bringing people to faith in Christ but also bringing them to maturity in Christ, through the work of the Holy Spirit within them, with his gifts, power, and fruit in their lives. Jesus stressed the teaching ministry of the Holy Spirit (John 14:25–26; 16:12–15), as did Paul (e.g., Col. 1:9) and John (1 John 2:20–27). The task of teaching within the church, then, participates in the process by which God himself brings his people to the fullness of maturity and Christlikeness. It is another way in which we share in the mission of God.

6. Third Lausanne Congress, "Cape Town Commitment," 1.10b.

Teaching is deeply rooted in the Bible. It was an essential part of the way God called, shaped, and "educated" his people Israel in the Old Testament. Professor Andrew Walls has called the Old Testament "the oldest and longest program of theological education."[7] For many generations God was teaching his people: teaching them through priests and prophets;[8] teaching them through the emerging Scriptures of the Torah, Psalms, and Wisdom literature; teaching them the truth about God, creation, humanity, sin, redemption, worship, and how to live as God's covenant people for the ultimate blessing of the nations. The psalmists recognized God as their prime teacher (e.g., Pss. 25:4–5, 8–9; 119:99). And parents were commanded to teach their children the great historical facts of their faith in order to learn the character of their God in his redeeming grace, global purpose, and covenant demands (e.g., Deut. 4:1–14; 6:1–9, 20–25). Teaching was supposed to be an integral part of the life of Old Testament Israel.

So it's not surprising that Jesus comes as a teacher. "Rabbi," they call him. From the moment he calls his disciples to be with him, he is teaching, teaching, teaching. Discipleship does not happen overnight. In his prayer to his Father, he says that he has taught them all he could, in a sense, of what the Father had given to him (John 17:6–8). And in his final words to them before his death, he promises that the Spirit would go on teaching them, just as he had done (John 16:12–15).

And what about the apostle Paul? We rightly think of him as a great missionary evangelist and church planter. But it is also clear that systematic scriptural teaching was integral to Paul's missional practice. He did it everywhere he could. Of course, sometimes he had to leave newly planted churches quickly, under threat (as in Philippi and Thessalonica), but even then he would write letters to them or send one of his companions to remind them of what he had managed to

---

7. In a lecture delivered at a mission leaders forum at the Overseas Ministries Study Center, New Haven, CT, April 27, 2012. (The Overseas Ministries Study Center is now housed at Princeton University.)

8. The prophets sometimes engaged in corrective teaching, lamenting the way the priests, who were actually ordained and commissioned to be teachers of the people, were failing in that task, with devastating spiritual and social results. See Lev. 10:10–11; Deut. 33:10 (about the tribe of Levi); Hos. 4:1–6 (ESV); Mal. 2:1–9.

teach them and to encourage them with further understanding. And whenever he had the opportunity, he stayed longer: in Corinth for eighteen months and in Ephesus for nearly three years. During those years in Ephesus, he transformed the tiny group of twelve disciples that he first found there (Acts 19:1–7) into a significant city church with several households and functioning elders—and he did it by systematic, hard-working teaching, both in a formal lecture setting and in house meetings. So he could make the double claim: "I have not hesitated to preach *anything that would be helpful to you* but have taught you publicly and from house to house," *and* "I have not hesitated to proclaim to you *the whole will of God*" (Acts 20:20, 27).

Those two verses give illuminating insight into Paul's preaching-teaching ministry. On the one hand, it was about "anything that would be helpful to you." That suggests what we might call "topical" preaching and teaching—addressing whatever issues were raised with him by these young believers, as we see him doing in his correspondence with the church in Corinth. On the other hand, he had proclaimed "the whole will [or plan] of God," which would mean a systematic explanation of the purposes of God since creation, based on the Old Testament Scriptures and climaxing in Christ and in God's cosmic, redemptive intention in the new creation—biblical exposition, in other words.

Naturally, Paul did not attempt to do all the teaching of all the churches himself. But he ensured that it was being done by others who were part of his missionary team, such as Timothy (2 Tim. 1:13–14; 2:1–2) or Titus (Titus 2:1–15). Or Apollos.

Apollos was a genuinely international, cross-cultural missionary teacher. He came from *Africa*, from the great city of Alexandria. He was a Jew and learned in the Scriptures (i.e., the Old Testament) and had come to faith in Jesus. He then went to *Asia* (Ephesus was the major metropolis of the Roman province of Asia), where he gained further theological education at the home of Priscilla and Aquila. And then he headed for *Europe*, to the Greek city of Corinth, where he launched a systematic teaching program. Here's how Luke describes the work of Apollos: "When he arrived [at Achaia], he was a great help to those who by grace had believed. For he vigorously refuted his Jewish opponents in public debate, proving from the

Scriptures that Jesus was the Messiah" (Acts 18:27–28). In terms of theological education, such as we now call it, Apollos was engaged in apologetics, Old Testament hermeneutics, and Christology!

Now here's the point that is relevant to mission. Later on, when the Christians in Corinth divided into factions, some boasting loyalty to Paul and others to Apollos, Paul refused to allow it. Yes, they had different gifts and ministries. Paul was an evangelistic church planter; Apollos was a theological church teacher. But they shared a common purpose. Paul insists that the evangelist (planter) and the teacher (waterer) share *a single mission*, a mission that they also share with God! He writes, "I planted the seed [*in evangelism*], Apollos watered it [*in his teaching*], but God has been making it grow. So neither the one who plants nor the one who waters is anything, but only God, who makes things grow. The one who plants and the one who waters have one purpose [literally in Greek, "they are one"], and they will each be rewarded according to their own labor. For we are co-workers in God's service; you are God's field, God's building" (1 Cor. 3:6–9).

Teaching within the church, then, in all its forms, is an *intrinsic* part of mission. That includes the conscientious work of a church pastor who teaches his people every week with faithful and applied biblical preaching, as well as the professor in a seminary crafting her courses, giving lectures, answering questions, setting tests, grading papers—all the labor of theological education, formal and informal. *Both* are obeying the Great Commission ("and teaching them . . .").

Speaking as one who has followed both callings (i.e., preaching in the church as an ordained pastor and teaching in seminary as an Old Testament professor), I feel a particular need to stress the missional nature of both callings and ministries. Pastors need to see that the Great Commission applies to them in their biblical teaching ministry, not just to the missionaries their churches may support overseas. And theological educators—whether in their own home country or in some cross-cultural context—likewise need to be seen and supported as partners in mission. Theological education is not merely ancillary, something that comes along after the "real mission" of church planting has been done. If we take Jesus seriously, teaching has to be included within our obedience to the Great Commission, not only in whatever form it takes but also wherever in the world it is done. I did not stop being a Great Commission "missionary" when I returned with my family from the seminary in India to go on teaching in a college in the UK. Only the geography changed. The missional task remained the same.

I recall a conversation I had with a woman in a church some time ago, after I had tried to explain the vision and work of Langham Partnership. I told her all about how we strive to strengthen evangelical theological education in the majority world by funding doctorates, to create and distribute much-needed Christian literature, and to train local pastors in the skills of biblical preaching. "Oh, so you're not really a missionary organization then," she concluded. I knew what she meant: Langham Partnership does not *send missionaries* from this country to somewhere else (though some of our staff do serve cross-culturally). But I felt like replying, "Of course we are! Haven't you read the Great Commission, line three: 'and *teaching them . . .* '?"

Teaching is an essential part of obedience to the Great Commission. The Cape Town Commitment articulates this significant role of theological education within the overall mission of the church globally. As one part of the teaching ministry of the church, theological education sits within the second of our five marks of mission and, along with evangelism, contributes essentially to building and maturing God's church.

> The mission of the Church on earth is to serve the mission of God, and the mission of theological education is to strengthen and accompany the mission of the Church. . . .
>
> Those of us who lead churches and mission agencies need to acknowledge that theological education is *intrinsically* missional. Those of us who provide theological education need to ensure that it is *intentionally* missional, since its place within the academy is not an end in itself, but to serve the mission of the Church in the world.[9]

So that completes the left side of our diagram—our task of building the church through evangelism and of discipling through teaching, the first and second marks of mission. We turn to the other side of the diagram in our next chapter.

9. Third Lausanne Congress, "Cape Town Commitment," 2F.4 (italics added).

6

Serving Society through Compassion and Justice

In chapter 5, our focus was on the church itself, enabling church growth in both numbers and maturity through evangelism and teaching—the first and second marks of mission. Now our focus shifts outward to our role in society, to the third and fourth marks of mission: responding to human need in acts of love and compassion and seeking to both enact and advocate for justice, reconciliation, and peace.

Where is *that* in the Great Commission?

Observing What Christ Commanded

There is no explicit mention of words like *compassion* and *justice* in Matthew 28, but I see them plainly implied in what Jesus says in verse 20: "teaching them to observe *all that I have commanded you*" (ESV). As we read the Gospels, we see that Jesus had plenty to say to his disciples about compassion and justice and about reconciliation and peacemaking. Obeying *all* that Jesus commanded must surely involve attending to all his teaching about radical love, generosity, care for the most despised, and all the other practical demands of living the transformed life of the kingdom of God—things that would imply or include what the third and fourth marks of mission refer to.

It is also worth noting that Jesus did not say "teaching them *all that I taught you*," as if it were only a matter of passing on his teachings, the truths that go into our heads. Don't misunderstand me. This is not to suggest that the *content* of Jesus's teaching is unimportant. Far from it! The fact that we have four Gospel records of his life, example and teaching, and death and resurrection shows how seriously his early followers took the responsibility of preserving and handing on the authentic record of his deeds and his words. Teaching the truth *of* Jesus and *about* Jesus was clearly of paramount importance to the apostles. But the Great Commission is not about that very necessary task alone, simply teaching others *what Jesus taught*.

No, Jesus said, "teaching them to *observe* [that is, keep or obey] all that I have *commanded* you." This makes the Great Commission very practical. It is a matter not just of transmitting cerebral doctrines but also of obeying ethical imperatives. This specific line within the Great Commission does two things.

First, it assumes that those who obey the primary command (to go and make disciples) will themselves be obeying all that Christ commanded, including all that he had to say about practical compassion and loving service in action. Mission has no integrity apart from the Christlike obedience of those who engage in it.

Second, it insists that part of the task of making disciples is to inculcate the same transformed and transforming obedience into the lives of those who are thus discipled, so that both those who are disciple-making *and* those who are being discipled are (as Paul would put it, echoing Jesus himself) "eager," "careful," and "devoted to doing good works" (Titus 2:14; 3:8, 14 AT). Both doing practical good works and teaching new disciples to be committed to such good works are unavoidably intrinsic to the plain meaning of Jesus's own words in the Great Commission.[1]

---

1. Ron Sider makes the same point emphatically in relation to the gospel itself, in the fullness of Jesus's own preaching and exemplifying the good news of the kingdom of God: "If the gospel is not just forgiveness but the Good News of the kingdom of God, we understand more clearly that ministering to both physical and spiritual needs of people is not some optional possibility, but essential to the gospel." See Ronald J.

Speaking of Paul, though he had planted many churches and written some letters before Matthew produced his record of Jesus's mandate on the Mount of Ascension, his driving ambition resonates strongly with the emphasis we are stressing here. This can be seen when we read (twice) that his missional goal was to bring about "the *obedience* of faith" among all nations (Rom. 1:5; 16:26 ESV). Indeed, Paul insisted that the gospel was something to be obeyed, not just believed (Rom. 15:18–19; 2 Cor. 9:13; 2 Thess. 1:8). This understanding of the gospel as a matter of obedience, not just belief, is shared by Peter (1 Pet. 4:17), James (James 2:14–26), John (1 John 2:3; 3:21–24; 5:1–3), and the writer to the Hebrews (Heb. 5:9); and, of course, it goes back to Jesus himself (e.g., Matt. 7:21–27; 28:20; Luke 11:28; John 14:23–24). The gospel that is intrinsically *verbal* (as an announcement of good news) is just as intrinsically *ethical* (as a demand for response).

So then, since the gospel itself *requires* obedience, and since the Great Commission mandates *teaching* obedience, mission that has any claim to be faithfully carrying out the Great Commission cannot just be about preaching a message and teaching the faith. It is about practical obedience to the lordship of Christ in every area of life in this world—practical obedience that is being modeled, taught, learned, and practiced. Or, in Christ's own words, it is about "observ[ing] all that I have commanded you." All of it.[2]

Sider, "What If We Defined the Gospel the Way Jesus Did?" in *Holistic Mission: God's Plan for God's People*, ed. Brian Woolnough and Wonsuk Ma, Regnum Edinburgh 2010 Series (Oxford: Regnum, 2010), 17–30, here 29. See also the excellent exposition by Scott W. Sunquist of the meaning of the gospel in the New Testament under the heading "An Intermission on Evangelism: What Is the Good News (*Euangelion*)?," in *Understanding Christian Mission: Participation in Suffering and Glory* (Grand Rapids: Baker Academic, 2013), 214–18.

2. It is intriguing that John Stott came to this understanding of the Great Commission in a way that changed the emphasis of his speaking and writing between 1966 and 1975. Whereas he had previously gone along with those who argued that the mission of the church, according to the Great Commission, was exclusively a "preaching, converting and teaching mission," he wrote in 1975, "Today . . . I would express myself differently. It is not just that the Commission includes the duty to teach baptised disciples everything Jesus had previously commanded . . . and that social responsibility is among the things that Jesus commanded. I now see more clearly that not only the consequences of the Commission but the actual Commission itself must be understood to include social as well as evangelistic responsibility, unless we

Compassion and Justice Together

Coming back to our third and fourth marks of mission, compassion and justice, is it justified to bracket them together as I have done, as a summary of the social dimension of Christian mission, implied and included in obeying all that Jesus commanded? I think it is, even though, of course, they are distinguishable.

Compassion speaks of actions motivated by deep human emotions of pity, genuine sympathy for the suffering, sick, and marginalized. It resonates with mercy, kindness, and practical love that reaches out and reaches down to help the needy, to heal the sick, to relieve poverty, to care for those struck by disasters, and so on.

Justice speaks of actions motivated by a deep human instinct for fairness. Some things are simply not right. We are offended and angered when people wantonly abuse, violate, exploit, enslave, or impoverish other people, especially when they "get away with it"—or worse, when such behaviors are institutionalized, normalized, legalized, and even legislated within the structures of society at national and international levels. There are those who, being wronged in such ways, long for justice for themselves. And there are those who actively seek justice on their behalf. Wrongdoing needs to be put right. And wherever possible, doing justice can result in reconciliation and peace building, though that is incredibly hard and painful work.

The proposal here is that acts of loving compassion and acts of reconciling justice do go together as powerfully significant ways in which the church in mission can serve society and can committedly do so under Christ's lordship and in legitimate obedience to the Great Commission. Two reasons support this combination.

The character of God. The God we meet in the Bible, especially in the Scriptures of Jesus and the apostles (our Old Testament), is the God who combines perfect love and perfect justice. He is loving in all his acts of justice, and he is just and righteous in all his acts of love. Compassion is the defining self-identity of Yahweh, and justice is the foundation of his throne. Here are some key, indicative verses:

---

are to be guilty of distorting the words of Jesus." John Stott and Christopher J. H. Wright, *Christian Mission in the Modern World*, 2nd ed. (Downers Grove, IL: IVP Books, 2015), 22–23.

And [the LORD] passed in front of Moses, proclaiming, "The LORD, the LORD, the compassionate and gracious God, slow to anger, abounding in love and faithfulness, maintaining love to thousands, and forgiving wickedness, rebellion and sin. Yet he does not leave the guilty unpunished." (Exod. 34:6–7)

> The LORD is gracious and compassionate,
>   slow to anger and rich in love.
> The LORD is good to all;
>   he has compassion on all he has made.
> . . . .
> The LORD is righteous in all his ways
>   and faithful in all he does. (Ps. 145:8–9, 17)

> The LORD reigns, let the earth be glad;
> . . . .
>   righteousness and justice are the foundation of his throne.
>   (Ps. 97:1–2)

> For I, the LORD, love justice. (Isa. 61:8)

> I will sing of your love and justice;
>   to you, LORD, I will sing praise. (Ps. 101:1)

The teaching of Jesus. Since the Great Commission comes at the end of Matthew's Gospel, we confine ourselves to Matthew's record of Jesus's teaching, where we find the same combination of loving compassion and mercy and commitment to justice. Sometimes they seem to coalesce. For example, we might think of almsgiving to the poor and needy as an example of "third mark" compassion. But Jesus explicitly describes it as "doing *righteousness*" (see Matt. 6:1–4). In doing so, he uses the same word (i.e., *dikaiosynē*) as in the fourth beatitude: "Blessed are those who hunger and thirst for *justice*" (Matt. 5:6 AT). The word is often translated "righteousness," and we have tended to confine that to the spiritual status of being right with God. It includes that, of course, but for Jesus and the Old Testament Scriptures (and in the language Jesus was speaking), the word meant not only a right relationship with God but also right, just, and fair relationships on earth. Righteousness-justice was not merely a status or an attribute; it was something you *do* or something you *long for*. Blessed are those who hunger and thirst for that, said Jesus. And the strong connection between justice and compassion comes in the very next beatitude: "Blessed are the merciful" (Matt. 5:7).

Jesus's contemporaries knew from their Scriptures that the reign of the God of Israel would bring justice and peace, so those who enter the kingdom of God through faith in Jesus must live in a way that enacts the justice of God's kingdom in the provisional here and now. For that is what brings anxiety-free security. "Seek first his kingdom and his righteousness [or justice]" (Matt. 6:33). And that is precisely what the Pharisees, for all their punctilious religious observance, were failing to do. So Jesus excoriates them as neither entering the kingdom of God themselves nor letting others do so, and then he goes on: "Woe to you, teachers of the law and Pharisees, you hypocrites! You give a tenth of your spices—mint, dill and cumin. But you have neglected the more important [literally "heavier," "weightier"] matters of the law—*justice, mercy and faithfulness*" (Matt. 23:23).

It seems likely that, in his choice of those three words to condense the "heavier" matters of the law, Jesus had in mind Micah's very similar triplet: "Do justice, love mercy, and walk humbly with your God" (Mic. 6:8 AT). Or possibly he had Zechariah's exhortation in view: "Administer true justice; show mercy and compassion to one another" (Zech. 7:9). For Jesus, as for the Prophets, showing compassion and doing justice *go together* as God-imitating responses to human suffering caused by human wrongdoing.[3]

Jesus modeled in life what he later commanded in the Great Commission—that is, he not only *taught* compassion; he *obeyed* what the Law and the Prophets required. "He was not afraid to look human need in the face, in all its ugly reality. And what he saw invariably moved him to compassion, and so to compassionate service. Sometimes he spoke. But his compassion never dissipated itself in words; it found expression in deeds. He saw, he felt, he acted. The movement was from the eye to the heart and from the heart to the

---

3. See also Damon So, "The Missionary Journey of the Son of God into the Far Country," in Woolnough and Ma, *Holistic Mission*, 47–58.

hand. His compassion was always aroused by the sight of need, and it always led to constructive action."[4]

One might add, by way of concluding this section, that the history of Christian mission shows how, again and again since the earliest centuries, followers of Jesus have intuitively reflected his compassion for the poor and needy, the sick and disabled, the ignorant and illiterate, the enslaved and imprisoned, the violated and abused, and so on—and have taken compassionate action to alleviate those conditions. This is not to say, of course, that they thought of or articulated those very practical and Christlike responses to human need by using the specific word *mission*. But that is somewhat beside the point. They certainly believed (and said) that they were acting in obedience to Christ's commands and following Christ's example—which merits us now using a word like *mission* to describe their actions, for they were certainly being purposefully obedient to the call of God and the mind of Christ.

What is also interesting is that, again and again, Christians who have felt moved to respond purposefully to human need in works of love and compassion (the third mark of mission) have also recognized the need to actively redress the factors that give rise to those conditions in the first place—usually some form of long-term injustice manifested in exploitative and oppressive systems and culturally deep-rooted inequalities. That is, they moved into the fourth mark of mission, seeking justice. Even as early as the fourth century, Christians in Asia Minor were advocating against slavery, and some were actively working to free slaves at considerable personal sacrifice. Early missionaries to India pioneered social and political campaigns to outlaw some of the more horrendous social practices they encountered there. At approximately the same time, members of the evangelical Clapham Sect in Britain were bending every political nerve and muscle in the prolonged fight against slavery and

4. John Stott, *Walk in His Shoes: The Compassion of Jesus* (Nottingham: Inter-Varsity, 1976), quoted in Jason Fileta, "Relentless Love and Justice in Radical Whole-Life Discipleship," in *Living Radical Discipleship: Inspired by John Stott*, ed. Laura S. Meitzner Yoder (Carlisle, UK: Langham Global Library, 2021), 64. In his essay, Fileta distinguishes between "Domesticated Love [That] Makes Justice a Project" and "Relentless Love [That] Integrates Justice into Every Aspect of Life."

other matters of social reform at home—unquestionably matters of justice. And today, alongside mission agencies that align with that third mark (compassion) are organizations that actively embrace the fourth (justice) as their *missional* calling, like Christian Solidarity and International Justice Mission, in relation to modern slavery and human trafficking.[5]

Let's return to the Great Commission.

Deuteronomy and the Great Commission

I said that the third and fourth marks of mission through which we serve society in the name of Christ are implied in the words of Jesus, that our disciple-making must include teaching new disciples to "observe all that I have commanded you," since Christ's commands certainly ranged into matters of compassion and justice. However, it is also worth hearing the scriptural echoes in that phrase itself: "observe [meaning to "keep," and obviously, therefore, to "obey"] all that I have commanded you." It is almost certainly a deliberate echo of Deuteronomy.[6]

In the book of Deuteronomy, Moses or God often address the Israelites in this way. Exhortations like "Be careful to follow every command I am giving you today" (Deut. 8:1) are frequent. It is very likely that the first disciples, hearing Jesus's words—especially after

---

5. To document the point being made in this paragraph would take another whole book, or several. Fortunately, there are plenty that make the case very thoroughly. Two older books still worth consulting for evangelical rationale and commitment to social engagement in compassion and justice are Stephen Charles Mott, *Biblical Ethics and Social Change* (New York: Oxford University Press, 1982), and Waldron Scott, *Bring Forth Justice: A Contemporary Perspective on Mission* (Grand Rapids: Eerdmans, 1980). On the long story of the church's constructive approach to issues of social and economic injustice, on the basis of the core beliefs of Christian faith and the message of Christ, see Tom Holland, *Dominion: How the Christian Revolution Remade the World* (New York: Basic Books, 2019), and John Dickson, *Bullies and Saints: An Honest Look at the Good and Evil of Christian History* (Grand Rapids: Zondervan, 2021). An excellent survey of the evangelical combination of evangelism and social action in the UK in the past three centuries is provided by Ian J. Shaw, *Evangelicals and Social Action: From John Wesley to John Stott* (London: Inter-Varsity, 2021).

6. This would not be surprising, since Jesus meditated deeply on Deuteronomy, quoting three times from chaps. 6 and 8 when tempted by Satan in the wilderness (see, e.g., Matt. 4:1–11).

his opening self-identification that also sounded very Deuteronomic (cf. Deut. 4:39)—would have picked up that echo. This is the Lord God of their Scriptures speaking!

In Deuteronomy it is very clear that God commanded Israel to reflect God's own character by "walking in his ways." Listen, for example, to Deuteronomy 10:12–19. After telling them what their God is like and who God most cares for, the text immediately tells the Israelites to do the same—to defend the familyless (doing justice) and care for the landless (practical compassion to foreigners): "For the LORD your God is God of gods and Lord of lords, the great God, mighty and awesome, who shows no partiality and accepts no bribes. He defends the cause of the fatherless and the widow, and loves the foreigner residing among you, giving them food and clothing. *And you are to love* those who are foreigners, for you yourselves were foreigners in Egypt" (Deut. 10:17–19).

This single example could be multiplied many times in Deuteronomy and indeed throughout the Old Testament Scriptures.[7] God wanted his people Israel to be *like God* by showing compassion and seeking justice for the poor and needy, for the homeless, the family-less, the landless. That was exactly what Yahweh had done for Israel itself when they were in need. In the exodus, God had demonstrated compassionate concern for the suffering Hebrew slaves and then exercised justice in delivering them from oppression. So God then commands the Israelites to embody such divine compassion and justice in their own social, political, and economic life: be like the God you worship! "Walking in the ways of the LORD" required nothing less than reflecting God's character and following his example.

So then, in the same way and in the same tone of voice, Jesus is effectively saying to his disciples, "Your mission is to make disciples and to teach them to obey what I have commanded you, which, as you know, is deeply rooted in all that God commanded his people in

---

7. I have explored this Yahweh-reflective nature of Old Testament ethics more thoroughly in *Old Testament Ethics for the People of God* (Downers Grove, IL: IVP Academic, 2004). For an even more detailed analysis, see David L. Baker, *Tight Fists or Open Hands? Wealth and Poverty in Old Testament Law* (Grand Rapids: Eerdmans, 2009).

our Scriptures, reflecting my Father's own character as the God of compassion and justice."

Light of the World

Out of this shared scriptural background comes Jesus's astonishing word to his disciples: "You are the light of the world" (Matt. 5:14). That must have come as a surprise to that odd bunch of people: a few fishermen, a tax collector, a former terrorist. What on earth did Jesus mean by such a sweeping metaphor? Did he mean that they would be preachers of the truth of the gospel and so bring gospel light to people in the darkness of ignorance and sin? Well, yes, of course, he would have included that in the overall task of the apostolic mission, and indeed on another occasion, he sent them out on a mission that included preaching the kingdom of God. That's how Paul uses the same metaphor: "For God, who said, 'Let light shine out of darkness,' made his light shine in our hearts to give us the light of the knowledge of God's glory displayed in the face of Christ" (2 Cor. 4:6). But look again at what Jesus actually stresses here when he explains what he means by "light": "Let your light shine before others, that they may see *your good deeds* and glorify your Father in heaven" (Matt. 5:16)—not "that they may hear your great preaching" but "see your good deeds." They *did have a message to preach*—of course they did. The good news of the kingdom of God must be told clearly in words if it is to be heard as "good news." I have stressed that repeatedly. But when Jesus talks about "light" here, he is speaking of *lives*, not just words. And he means lives that are *attractive*[8]—by being filled with goodness, mercy, love, compassion, and justice.

Once again, Jesus is drawing on a strong Old Testament tradition. God had called *Israel* to be a "light to the nations." If they would live according to the laws God gave them, then something of the quality of their lives as a society would attract curiosity at the very least among other nations (Deut. 4:6–8). Being "light" had

8. The Greek word translated as "good" in "good deeds" is *kalos*, which also means "beautiful," not just "morally upright."

a strongly ethical and social meaning. Isaiah combines "light" and "righteousness" rhetorically and powerfully:

> Is not this the kind of fasting I have chosen:
> to loose the chains of injustice
>   and untie the cords of the yoke,
> to set the oppressed free
>   and break every yoke?
> Is it not to share your food with the hungry
>   and to provide the poor wanderer with shelter—
> when you see the naked, to clothe them,
>   and not to turn away from your own flesh and blood?
> Then *your light* will break forth like the dawn,
>   and your healing will quickly appear;
> then *your righteousness* will go before you.
> . . . .
> If you spend yourselves in behalf of the hungry
>   and satisfy the needs of the oppressed,
> then *your light* will rise in the darkness,
>   and your night will become like the noonday. (Isa. 58:6–8,
>   10)

Light shines from people who are committed to compassion and justice and show it in practice. And that kind of light, as Isaiah continues a little later, reflects the light of *God's own presence and glory* among his people. It is the light of God, seen in the lives of his people, that will draw the nations.

> Arise, shine, for your light has come,
>   and the glory of the Lord rises upon you.
> See, darkness covers the earth
>   and thick darkness is over the peoples,
> but the Lord rises upon you
>   and his glory appears over you.
> Nations will come to your light,
>   and kings to the brightness of your dawn. (Isa. 60:1–3)

The light of such God-reflective and God-imitating good deeds of loving justice is *missionally attractive*. It will bring people to glorify the living God. Isn't that exactly what Jesus said? That is why it is legitimate to speak of the third and fourth marks as marks of *mission*. They are not just doing good stuff because Christians ought to be nice people. They bring glory to God because they reflect the character of God, and in doing so they bring others to glorify God also, which is intrinsic to the mission of God.

The third and fourth marks of mission constitute a kind of *missional magnetism*.

So, then, in the *Old Testament*, God commands Israel to be a people committed to practical, down-to-earth exercise of compassion and justice, in ways that would reflect and embody God's own character—Yahweh, the God who cares for the poor and needy, who defends the cause of the widow and orphan.

And *Jesus* both endorses that mandate for his disciples and then, in the Great Commission, commands them to pass it on to the new disciples they make, by "teaching them to observe all that [he has] commanded [them]."

And they did.

The New Testament Church

We know, of course, the exciting story of the expansion of the early church in the book of Acts. We marvel at how the church grew and spread in all directions through evangelism and church planting. The first and second marks of mission were very evident among them! But we should not overlook how the apostles and those first communities of Jesus followers showed a strong commitment to this other dimension of the Great Commission—obeying what Jesus himself had taught about social and economic compassion and justice.

Luke tells us twice that the earliest community of Jesus followers in Jerusalem sought to work out their *spiritual* unity through *economic* sharing. And while this "giving to anyone who had need" was primarily a means of relieving poverty among themselves, it may well have reached out in generosity to others in Jerusalem, since Luke records that, for a while at least, they were "enjoying the favor of all the people" (Acts 2:45, 47).

All the believers were one in heart and mind. No one claimed that any of their possessions was their own, but they shared everything they had. With great power the apostles continued to testify to the resurrection of the Lord Jesus. And God's grace was so powerfully at work in them all that *there were no needy persons among them*. For from time to time those who owned land or houses sold them, brought the money from the sales and put it at the apostles' feet, and it was distributed to anyone who had need. (Acts 4:32–35)

What is very interesting is that, whether consciously or not, they were fulfilling yet another word of God in Deuteronomy. At least Luke seems to think so. For when he says "there were no needy persons among them," he is repeating almost word for word the Greek translation of Deuteronomy 15:4, where God says, "*There need be no poor people among you*, for in the land the LORD your God is giving you to possess as your inheritance, he will richly bless you, if only you fully obey the LORD your God and are careful to follow all these commands I am giving you today"[9] (Deut. 15:4–5; the word Luke chooses in Acts 4:34, *endeēs*, is the same word, out of several possible Greek words for "poor," as in Deut. 15:4 LXX).

What about the apostle Paul?

We usually refer to Paul's first missionary journey as the one he made with Barnabas when they were sent by the church in Antioch, after a word from the Holy Spirit, to preach the gospel and plant churches in Asia Minor in Acts 13. But actually, the *first* time Barnabas and Saul of Tarsus were *sent* by the church in Antioch after a word from the Holy Spirit was when they took a gift to the church in Jerusalem in anticipation of the coming famine in Acts 11:27–30. Paul's first missionary journey was for famine relief! And, says Luke, "when Barnabas and Saul had finished their mission,[10] they

9. Those closing words of Deut. 15:5 are another example of that Deuteronomic turn of phrase that Jesus picks up in the Great Commission, when he speaks of "teaching them to *obey everything I have commanded you*" (Matt. 28:20).

10. The Greek word here is *diakonia*, often translated "service" or sometimes "ministry." Significantly, it is the same word used three times in Acts 6, both for the daily distribution of food to widows and for the preaching of the word. Unfortunately, the NIV obscures this equivalence by inserting "ministry" before "the word" in v. 2 (where it is not present in Greek), while translating the verb form, *diakoneō*, as "*wait on* tables," which sounds inferior (preachers seem more important than

returned from Jerusalem [to Antioch], taking with them John, also called Mark" (Acts 12:25). And it was after that first mission that the Holy Spirit instructs the church to send the same pair, Barnabas and Saul (and initially John Mark as well), for further work in more distant parts (Acts 13:1–3).

I think that first mission trip made such a big impression on Paul that caring for the poor became part of his mission and teaching from then on. How do I know that? Well, because he tells us! In the second chapter of what was probably his earliest letter, Galatians, Paul describes a most significant moment in his missionary career, when he went to Jerusalem again to meet with the other apostles there. They accepted and endorsed his ministry of preaching the gospel among the gentiles, agreeing that God had entrusted that to Paul and Barnabas, just as Peter and others were primarily bringing the gospel to their fellow Jews. And to seal that agreement, they granted to Paul and Barnabas "the right hand of fellowship." Then Paul adds this revealing comment: "All they asked was that we should continue to remember the poor, the very thing I had been eager to do all along" (Gal. 2:10). Paul implies, "They didn't have to ask me to do that; I was doing it already!"[11] As Verlyn Verbrugge and Keith Krell conclude,

---

waiters—which is not what the apostles were saying). A literal rendering of the passage would run as follows: "Their widows were being overlooked in the daily *ministry* [*diakonia*; assumed to be distribution of food]. . . . 'It is not right for us, neglecting the word of God, to *minister at* [*diakonein*] tables. . . . We will give our attention to . . . the *ministry* [*diakonia*] of the word'" (vv. 1, 2, 4). Clearly both actions counted as "ministry," and both required people filled with the Holy Spirit. One was social (the *diakonia* of food); the other was spiritual (the *diakonia* of the word). The apostles knew what *their* priority and calling was. But not everybody in the church was (or is!) an apostle. So they took action to ensure that other people were prayerfully appointed for whom the other ministry was *their* priority and anointing. In our terms, we could say that the apostles made sure that *the church as a whole* was fulfilling the first, second, and third marks of mission, without allowing any to dominate or marginalize the other.

11. There is a possible alternative reading of the tense of the verb Paul uses here, which could imply that it was only after the Jerusalem apostles asked Paul to remember the poor that he began to do so. But in a very thorough analysis, Verlyn Verbrugge and Keith Krell come to the conclusion that the NIV renders the correct sense of what Paul wrote. See *Paul and Money: A Biblical and Theological Analysis of the Apostle's Teachings and Practices* (Grand Rapids: Zondervan, 2015), 122–29.

At whatever time the conference reported in Gal 2:1–10 took place, Paul had already been involved in projects for the poor—first as a Pharisee, and then as a leader of the Jesus movement in Antioch and elsewhere. As he established churches in Asia Minor and later in Macedonia and Achaia and he encountered poverty, he was indeed eager to help the poor out (if in no other way, by working for a living and not being a burden to them), and he encouraged his churches to do the same. This is what the Lord Jesus would expect of him, for this is what Jesus himself did when he was on earth.[12]

For Paul, then, practical care for the poor was an integral part of his missionary work alongside preaching and teaching. It was integrated into his evangelistic and church-planting work. Indeed, one might argue that Paul learned from the early example set by the Jerusalem apostles in Acts 6. He knew, of course, that his own apostolic calling was primarily to preach the gospel and teach the Word. But he ensured that trustworthy and Christ-honoring people were chosen and appointed to administer the collection among the Greek churches for the poor in Jerusalem. That occupied so much of his attention. This is clear in 1 Corinthians 16:1–4 and 2 Corinthians 8. And significantly, he describes this whole project as his *diakonia* for the saints (Rom. 15:25). Paul embraced and embodied all of the first three marks of mission.

There is even a hint of the fourth mark, though not in a modern sense of working for justice in the political system—an option that was not open to Christians in the Roman Empire other than through prayer for those in authority to do so (Rom. 13:1–7; 1 Tim. 2:1–2). Within the polycentric Christian community, and especially between Jewish- and gentile-background believers, Paul saw the need for a kind of fairness in which the wealth of some could be mobilized to bring "equality" in the face of the poverty of others. The word he uses twice as his goal is *isotēs*, the regular Greek word for "equality," for which we might read in this context "a just balance" (2 Cor. 8:13–14). In a similar vein, he sees the gentile gift to the Jerusalem church as a kind of paying off of a debt, a material gift as owed for the spiritual blessing of the gospel (Rom. 15:27).

12. Verbrugge and Krell, *Paul and Money*, 129.

Within or beyond the Church?

At this point, an objection is frequently raised: This challenge to exercise love, compassion, and generosity is primarily intraecclesial—that is, it is a matter of Christians showing familial love *to one another in practical ways within the church*, not a matter of serving society beyond the church in such ways. Paul collected money for the benefit of poor Christians; he did not start charities for the wider society. We should, of course, do the first, but the second—*public* acts of compassion and concern for social justice—are no part of the church's mission. So it is said.

There are several biblical responses to this objection. First, remember that our argument throughout this book is that we need the whole Bible to inform our theology and practice of mission. So we cannot limit ourselves to the practice of the first generation of Christian churches in the New Testament alone. We have seen the strong emphasis on social compassion and justice in the Old Testament based on the character and commands of God himself and also how much Jesus's own teaching was rooted in those Scriptures. And as we stressed above, Israel was called into existence to be "a light to the nations," *to be a model or paradigm of what God wants for human society among the nations.* So, from a purely hermeneutical point of view, as regards the very purpose of Israel's existence, we cannot confine the Old Testament's commands in this area of social compassion and justice to having relevance either to Israel alone or to the church alone. They are indicative, or paradigmatic, of what "the Judge of all the earth" requires. Or, simply, if that is what God demanded of Israel, it is because that is what God requires of humanity—and how much more, therefore, is what God expects from those whose humanity is being restored in Christ to the true image of God. Societal compassion and justice, so integral to God's command to Old Testament Israel, cannot simply be airbrushed out of Christ's mandate for the Israel of God in the Messiah Jesus.

Second, Jesus rejected the idea that good works of various kinds should be confined to "one's own people." That, he pointed out, was a mark of the pagan gentile world. What should uniquely distinguish citizens of God's kingdom in obedience to Christ and imitation of his Father should be loving care and generosity precisely to those *outside* the fold of his own disciples, even for enemies (Matt. 5:43–48). And, indeed, it was exactly that feature of Christ-obedient behavior in times of frightening pandemics in the Roman Empire that so impressed pagan observers—the Christians (to the amazement of the pagans) tended not only to their own sick but also to others. To limit the third and fourth marks of mission to within the church itself, rather than including how we show the love of God's kingdom in the wider society, seems quite contrary to the explicit teaching of Jesus, teaching that was certainly not interpreted in that way by his followers in the early centuries.

Third, while Paul obviously did stress the importance of mutual care and generosity between and among fellow believers, he sets that care within the wider obligation of doing good to all. "Therefore, as we have opportunity, let us do good to *all* people, *especially* to those who belong to the family of believers" (Gal. 6:10). Especially, not exclusively.

And this is no isolated text, by way of concession. The strongest evidence that Paul expected Christians to be engaged in what we are calling the third and fourth marks of mission is in his letter to Titus.

The context of this small letter is important. Titus had been left in Crete, presumably after Paul's evangelistic and church-planting efforts on the island. Crete was a notorious den of iniquity, full of pirates and gangsters, such that Paul could quote a contemporary opinion without fear of contradiction: "One of Crete's own prophets [i.e., Epimenides] has said it: 'Cretans are always liars, evil brutes, lazy gluttons'" (Titus 1:12). What hope was there for any change in such a society? Well, according to Paul, it would come through "knowledge of *the truth that leads to godliness*" (Titus 1:1).

As we said before, the truth of the gospel is ethically transformative. It "leads to godliness" here and now, not just to heaven when you die. The convincing proof of the truth of the gospel would be when the world (even in Crete and its modern equivalents) sees those who *believe* the gospel *transformed* by it in the way they live in full public view. So the specific responsibility of pastors and elders when the church gathers is to *teach* this applied gospel, this "truth that leads to godliness," in such a way that they equip their people in what it means to live a gospel-transformed life. That is the repeated thrust of Titus 2. And that new life must include *publicly visible good works.*

Six times in this short letter Paul urges the importance of good works as the proof of faith and the fruit of the gospel of grace (Titus 2:11–14; 3:4–8). And it is clear that this means public good, not just personal uprightness. This is godliness in the form of good works that are visible and for the benefit of the outside world, not confined to Christians caring only for one another.

Let's unpack that phrase "the truth that leads to godliness" in the way Paul applies it. By "the truth" he obviously means the gospel itself. And he makes it clear that the salvation we receive as gospel truth is entirely a matter of God's grace and explicitly *not* based on any good works or righteousness of our own (Titus 3:5–6). But the grace that *saves* us then also and immediately *teaches* us to live out the kind of "godliness" that is eager and devoted to good works (2:12–14; 3:8). What then must Titus do if he is to finish the task that Paul had begun (1:5)? As well as appointing elders, he must teach, teach, teach.[13] And what he is to teach is not simply the gospel itself (in evangelism) but the practically applied outworking of the gospel for every category of believer (old and young, men and women). And such applied teaching, if followed, would have missional impact in the public sphere. Christian lives changed by the gospel (lives of godliness and good works) would be visible in such a way that would (negatively) disarm opposition (2:5) and (positively) commend the gospel of salvation (2:9–10).

Furthermore, the terms Paul uses again and again[14] were commonly applied to public benefactors, people who earned social approval and

---

13. The word occurs eight times in the NIV translation of Titus 2, which is more than in the Greek, but the word is implied in the sequence of accusatives of those who are to be the object of Titus's teaching.

14. In three short chapters, Paul uses *kala erga* ("good works," the same phrase as in Jesus's "light of the world" saying) four times (2:7, 14; 3:8, 14) and uses *pan ergon agathon* ("every good work") twice (1:16; 3:1). The NIV's translation "what is good" seems rather weak, lacking the concrete specificity of good *works.* Similarly, "Do what is right" (Rom. 13:3b) is "Do good" (*to agathon poiei*). "In the Roman world, 'doing good' was the language of benefaction and public service. Ordinarily, it would be the duty of the rich and powerful to promote the city's welfare through acts of public service. But here Paul turns cultural expectations on their head. He urges, not the power brokers, but the powerless Christian community, to take on the role

honor for doing civic good. Christian believers, urges Paul, must be eager and devoted to such public service.[15] Their kindness, gentleness, compassion, fairness, truthfulness, self-control, and honesty would stand out in a culture of lying, greed, and bestial evil. And that in itself would have *missional impact*, even by Christian slaves in their degrading workplaces. The third and fourth marks of mission, in addition to their intrinsic value (it is simply good to do good), can have remarkable apologetic and evangelistic power. We could illustrate the same point from 1 Peter, where Christians are repeatedly urged to be "doers of good" in the public arena (whether they suffer for it or not—indeed, especially if they do).[16]

So the idea that Christian works of compassion or social righteousness should be *confined* to believers in the church (though, of course, they ought to be *modeled* there) would simply not have occurred to Paul or to other Christ followers in the centuries following him. And there are plenty of other passages that emphasize the importance of such care for the needy, such as 1 Timothy 6:17–19; James 2:14–17; and 1 John 3:17–18.

It seems to me that Jesus and his apostles would all have agreed with the simple affirmation of Proverbs 29:7: "The righteous care about justice for the poor, but the wicked have no such concern."

For all these biblical reasons, then, I am firmly convinced that gospel-centered social engagement in the world, under the lordship of Christ and bearing witness to the kingdom of God, is a legitimate, indeed an indispensable, dimension of Christian mission, if we are to be obedient to the Great Commission as a whole and with all the depth of its biblical roots and echoes. I find it exegetically illogical

---

of public benefactor. 'Doing good' is thus redefined in terms of performing acts of humble love and service. It becomes part of the church's transforming witness in the public square." Dean Flemming, *Recovering the Full Mission of God: A Biblical Perspective on Being, Doing and Telling* (Downers Grove, IL: IVP Academic, 2013), 189.

15. And they were. For a most instructive account of early Christian engagement in public benefaction (the word is simply Latin for "good doing"!), see Bruce W. Winter, *Seek the Welfare of the City: Christians as Benefactors and Citizens* (Grand Rapids: Eerdmans, 1996).

16. For a thorough exposition of this emphasis in 1 Peter, see Dean Flemming, "Mission from the Margins: Being, Doing and Telling in 1 Peter," in *Recovering the Full Mission of God*, 209–29.

and, speaking for myself, impossible to think that the Great Commission narrowly specifies the ministries of evangelism and teaching as the *sole* legitimate tasks of the church's mission. "Teaching them to observe *all that I have commanded you*" cannot *merely* mean "teaching them to evangelize and to teach others" (though, of course, it includes that), since that is by no means "all" that Jesus commanded his disciples to observe. As we have seen, the early church and the apostle Paul certainly did not think that missional obedience to Christ and the gospel meant only that.

We are called to the *integration* of faith and works, of word and deed, of the proclamation and demonstration of the gospel.

So let us hold them together as integrally and necessarily belonging to each other, and refrain from perpetuating an unbiblical and unhealthily competing dichotomy. Scott Sunquist sums it up well:

> For the past century or so, it was common to talk about two distinct but essential elements of Christian mission: evangelism and justice. Such an approach is misleading. Since evangelism is about Jesus, and Jesus was an integrated whole human being, it makes no sense to give a dichotomous reading of Jesus's love for humanity. Jesus's love covers our deepest personal needs and the greatest social injustices. In fact, as we all know, they are of the same fabric. . . . So, in evangelism, we start with a single quality of God in Jesus Christ—love—rather than starting with a dichotomy of word and works, or evangelism and justice, or preaching and social justice.
>
> We should be a little suspicious if a person talks about "both sides" of the life of Jesus. In the past it was common to use such language, to talk about the mission of God as two dance partners (evangelism and social justice) or as two sides of the same coin. But these analogies are not just inadequate, they are misleading. Jesus was a whole person, filled to overflowing with the kenotic, self-emptying love of God. . . . His love is as personal as his forgiveness of those who killed him, and it is as large as his suffering for the sins of the world.[17]

17. Sunquist, *Understanding Christian Mission*, 320.

7

The Goodness and Glory
of Creation

We come now to the third of our three major focal points of missional commitment, as we seek to integrate the "five marks of mission" around the lordship of Christ. In chapter 5 we considered the left side of our diagram (see fig. 7.1)—building *the church* through evangelism and teaching, the first and second marks of mission. Then, in chapter 6, we moved to the right side—serving *society* through works of compassion and justice, the third and fourth marks of mission. And so to the fifth mark we turn: our responsible and godly use of and care for *creation*.[1]

Where is *that* in the Great Commission?

1. Much more detailed expositions of the biblical teaching on creation, expansions of the material in these two chapters, and further discussion of our missional responsibility in the use of and care for creation can be found in the relevant chapters of three of my books and in the bibliography in each of them: Christopher J. H. Wright, *Old Testament Ethics for the People of God* (Downers Grove, IL: IVP Academic, 2004), chaps. 3 and 4; *The Mission of God: Unlocking the Bible's Grand Narrative* (Downers Grove, IL: IVP Academic, 2006), chap. 12; and *The Mission of God's People: A Biblical Theology of God's People*, Biblical Theology for Life (Grand Rapids: Zondervan, 2010), chaps. 3 and 15.

Fig. 7.1. Church, Society, Creation

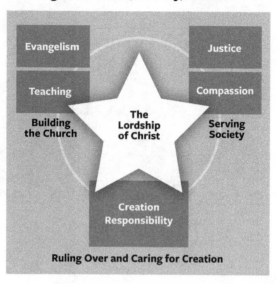

Well, actually, we could have started with creation, since it's where Jesus starts in the Great Commission. We have already emphasized that the Great Commission does not begin with a command but with an affirmation: "All authority in heaven and on earth has been given to me." Now that familiar combination, "heaven and earth," was the typical Jewish, Old Testament way of referring to the whole of creation.

It's not only where Jesus starts, of course; it's also where the Bible starts ("In the beginning God created the heavens and the earth"; Gen. 1:1). And it's where the Bible ends ("Then I saw 'a new heaven and new earth'"; Rev. 21:1). The whole mission of God in the great drama of Scripture runs from creation to new creation, as we saw in chapter 2, with all the implications of such a missional hermeneutic that we explored in chapter 3. And here, more than anywhere else, it is so important to read the words of Scripture—to hear the words of Jesus—in the flow of that great narrative.

For here is Jesus standing right at the center of the whole drama of Scripture, the capstone of the great canonical arc from Genesis to Revelation, claiming to be Lord over it all from beginning to end. Jesus is about to ascend to his Father's right hand, but he makes it very clear that he will not just be "up in heaven." Jesus is Lord of heaven *and earth*, the Lord of all creation.

Once again, it is Deuteronomy that provides the scriptural echo chamber for the astonishing claim that Jesus makes in Matthew 28:18. Listen to Moses talking to the Israelites about Yahweh in Deuteronomy 4: "Acknowledge and take to heart this day that the LORD is God *in heaven above and on the earth below*. There is no other" (Deut. 4:39). Yahweh, the Lord God of Israel, is God of heaven and earth (that is, he is Creator, Owner, and Ruler of the whole creation). This is the truth about the God of Israel that the Old Testament repeats all over the place, especially in the Psalms. And Jesus, standing on the Mount of Ascension, calmly takes that cosmic truth about the God revealed in Scripture—the God whom all Jesus's followers knew and worshiped as the Lord God of hosts, the Creator of the ends of the earth—and claims that identity and status for himself.

It's not surprising that when the disciples meet Jesus on the Mount of Ascension, they worship him (Matt. 28:16–17), though Matthew also points out with frank honesty that some doubt. But those who worship him could only have done so as Jews, because they were now utterly convinced that, as they bowed before the crucified and risen Christ, they were in the presence of the living God, the Holy One of Israel, the Maker of heaven and earth, the Lord of all creation.

So whatever our mission may include as we obey the Great Commission in multiple ways, it presupposes and is authorized by the cosmic truth that Jesus is Lord of all creation, that the earth belongs to him. Wherever we may go on this planet, we are walking on his "property." He is the landlord and we are his tenants. The earth exists under God's ownership, and we are stewards of it, accountable *to Christ himself* for what we do on the earth and with the earth. So we cannot separate our personal submission to Jesus Christ as Lord from our social and economic practice of living in, making use of, and caring for the creation that belongs to him, the Lord of heaven and earth.

At this point we must acknowledge that there are those who, while affirming the biblical logic of that last paragraph, would not feel they can include creation care as such in their understanding of *the mission of the church*. They may well have come to accept the integration of evangelism and social action, as in the classic documents of

Lausanne in 1974 and 1989. They affirm the validity of *four* of the marks of mission—evangelism, teaching, compassion, and justice. But to include creation care as a fifth mark of biblically legitimized Christian mission? They remain unconvinced.

Now we could easily try to justify the inclusion of the fifth mark on pragmatic grounds—that is, by pointing to the urgency of some of the destructive realities facing our world today, such as the accelerating loss of species (labeled by biologists as "the third great extinction"); the destruction of tropical forests; the pollution and warming of the oceans and melting of the polar ice caps; the devastation of natural habitats, which is increasing the likelihood of zoonotic diseases such as COVID-19 crossing from animals to humans; and the terrible injustices that climate chaos is wreaking on the poorest and most vulnerable of earth's inhabitants.

The realities and the needs are enormous, pressing, and urgent. And historically, over the centuries, the church has made powerful missional responses to urgent human needs and crises (disease, famine, ignorance and illiteracy, slavery, refugees, war, etc.), so there is plenty of precedent for Christians taking seriously, and as a matter of mission theology and practice, how we should be responding to this contemporary reality that faces the human race—the urgency of environmental and climatic breakdown.

Our affirmation of the lordship of Christ over the earth also affects the way we think about the actual places where we and others live. People and places are connected to one another within the purposes of God. Both the Old Testament (Gen. 10; Deut. 2; 32:8) and Paul (Acts 17:24–26) affirm God's sovereign distribution of the earth to peoples and God's overall involvement in their migrations too. God is interested and involved in the physical locations and environments of people's lives. Ecology is much more than merely having a sentimental love of nature, enjoying nice views, and saving endangered species. It is intimately connected to human well-being also. Comprehensive care for other people (loving one's neighbor, in its biblical breadth) includes care for their physical environment and whatever enhances or threatens it. It is a logical extension of the long-accepted view that our mission should attend to people's physical, intellectual, and spiritual needs (in medical, educational, evangelistic, and pastoral ministries), since all three of those dimensions of human need will be affected, for good or ill, by the quality of the environment in which people live.

In this chapter and the next, however, I simply want to take us back to the Bible and outline the foundations of a thoroughly biblical theology of creation. Since we are trying to ground a missional hermeneutic in the grand narrative of Scripture, we shall go back to the beginning of the Bible in this chapter and consider the goodness of creation and the glory of creation, especially as portrayed in the Old Testament. There are many urgent, empirical reasons why we as human beings should use and care for creation responsibly and restrain our destructive habits. But *as Christians* we have an enhanced motivation to do so, which is decidedly missional in its implications, since we discern in the goodness and glory of *creation* the goodness and glory of the *God* we love and serve. Our response to *it* expresses and exposes our response to *him*.

In chapter 8, we shall move to the other end of the biblical narrative and consider the eschatological goal of creation. We saw in chapter 3 that our understanding of mission is governed not only by looking back to the Great Commission of Christ that drives us forward but also by looking forward to the "end of the story"—the eschatological vision that draws us onward. A missional hermeneutic based on the great story (as well as the Great Commission) means that we live now in act 5 of the biblical narrative, shaped by the historical facts of acts 1–4 and by anticipation of the ultimate climax of the story in acts 6–7. And that applies just as much to our view of the earth and to the issue of creational responsibility and care. What we believe about the *ultimate destiny* of our planet will massively affect what we think we should be doing on it and with it in the present. Wrong or defective theology on this point can have—and is already having—disastrously deadly results.

The Goodness of Creation

Creation is good. That is the unmistakable message of the opening chapter of the Bible—act 1 of the drama of Scripture. Six times God declares that what he has just done is "good," and the seventh time he declares it "very good." We can think of this goodness of creation in two ways—in relation to God and in relation to ourselves—and in each case there are several things to be said.

Creation Is Good in Relation to God

THE GOOD CREATION REVEALS THE GOOD GOD

In other ancient Near Eastern cosmologies, creation is described as the work of multiple deities, in varying degrees of conflict and malevolence. By contrast, in the Old Testament, creation is the work of the one living God, Yahweh, and therefore it bears witness to that one God's existence, power, and character. For example, creation itself reveals the glory of God (Ps. 19:1–4); the righteousness of God (Ps. 50:6); the joyful care of God (Ps. 65:9–12); the abundant provision of God (Ps. 104:27–30); the kindness of God (Acts 14:17); and the power and deity of God (Rom. 1:20).

We encounter the living God in creation, though the creation is not God, just as we "hear" Beethoven in one of his symphonies, though the symphony is not "him"—or just as we "see" Rembrandt in one of his paintings, though he is not "in" the painting itself. The artist is recognizable in the works of his hands. So it is with the ultimate artist—the Maker of heaven and earth.

CREATION RECEIVES ITS INTRINSIC VALUE FROM GOD

"God saw that it was good," we are told repeatedly in Genesis 1. This is a statement about God's evaluation of his handiwork, which is quite independent of us human beings. In fact, it is stated six times before we even appear in the narrative, which means that it does not express *our* human response to the beauty or benefits of creation (though it certainly should, now that we are here!); rather, it expresses *God's* evaluation of his whole creation. It is the seal of God's approval on the whole universe in all its functioning parts. Creation has intrinsic value because it is valued by God, who is the source of all value. To speak of the goodness of creation is not, first of all, to say that it is *valuable to us* (though, of course, it is) but is to say that it is *valued by God* and was created "fit for purpose"—that is, for God's purpose.

One illustration of this is the way Psalm 104 celebrates not only those aspects of creation that directly serve human needs (crops and domestic animals) but also those that are of no immediate benefit to human life, at least from the perspective of the ancient world—the wild places of the earth (the tall trees and high mountains) and the wild creatures that live there (beasts of the forest, lions, whales, and so on). They are noticed, celebrated, and valued simply by being and doing what God created them to be and do. And God enjoys them as they do so!

CREATION IS OWNED BY GOD

"The earth is the LORD's, and everything in it" (Ps. 24:1). "To the LORD your God belong the heavens, even the highest heavens, the earth and everything in it" (Deut. 10:14). It is easy for us to get so used to verses like this that we casually underestimate how staggering and, in the polytheistic world of the ancient Near East, how countercultural such universal affirmations were. The whole universe (including this earth), they claim, is the property of Yahweh, the God of Israel. It all belongs to this one God. Our God.

The earth, then, lies under God's ownership—not ours. God is the supreme landlord. We are God's tenants, living by God's permission in what belongs to the Creator.[2] This biblical truth generates huge ethical implications in the economic and ecological realms that we cannot fully explore here. Fundamentally, it insists that we are accountable to God for how we treat his property. Such creational accountability is "the logical outworking of our love for God by caring for what belongs to him. 'The earth is the Lord's and everything in it.' The earth is the property of the God we claim to love and obey. We care for the earth, most simply, because it belongs to the one whom we call Lord."[3]

CREATION IS GOD'S TEMPLE

In the world of the ancient Near East, temples were envisaged as (literally) "microcosms"—that is, they were small representations

2. Or, as I once saw in the bathroom of a hotel room, "We are all guests on this planet." This sign did not specify, however, whose guests we are—that is, who the planet's owner is!

3. Third Lausanne Congress, "The Cape Town Commitment: A Confession of Faith and a Call to Action" (Lausanne Movement, 2011), 1.7a, https://lausanne.org/content/ctc/ctcommitment#capetown.

on earth of the shape and order of the cosmos itself. Their layout and shape and structures were an attempt to portray on a horizontal plane what was believed about the universe (land, sea, and sky) on a vertical plane.

Conversely, the cosmos as a whole could be seen as a "macro-temple"—that is, as the dwelling place of the gods. The gods "lived" in the heavens, as it were, but placed their images (statues) in the earthly temples that embodied their presence and their rule over their earthly domains.

This way of thinking about the relationship between the cosmos and temples is reflected in Old Testament Israel. The tabernacle in the wilderness and later the temple in Jerusalem modeled the cosmic union of heaven and earth—a microcosm of the presence and governance of the one living God, Yahweh. At the same time, from the converse perspective, God's declaration at each stage that his work of creation was "good" expressed his approval of the whole creation as a kind of cosmic temple, functioning in all its ordered complexity both as the place where he would install his "image" (humankind) and as the place he prepared for his own dwelling. "Heaven is my throne, and the earth is my footstool" (Isa. 66:1), God announces. That is temple language.[4] And as we saw at the end of chapter 2, this temple imagery runs right through to the final, great act 7 of the drama of Scripture, in which John's vision in Revelation 21–22 portrays the whole creation, a unified heaven and earth, as the ultimate and eternal dwelling place of God and his redeemed people from all nations, such that no physical temple will be needed therein.

How we behave on this earth and how we treat the earth itself, then, should be governed by the same sense of joy mixed with awe in the presence of holiness that was expected of the Israelites as they assembled in the courts of the temple. "Worship the LORD in the splendor of his holiness" (Ps. 96:9) is an exhortation that should

---

4. See especially John H. Walton, *The Lost World of Genesis One: Ancient Cosmology and the Origins Debate* (Downers Grove, IL: IVP Academic, 2009); G. K. Beale, *The Temple and the Church's Mission: A Biblical Theology of the Dwelling Place of God*, New Studies in Biblical Theology 15 (Downers Grove, IL: IVP Academic, 2004).

impact our attitudes and actions toward creation, not just our behavior in church.

The Bible constantly speaks of the natural world in relation to God. Creation obeys God's ordering, reveals God's glory, benefits from God's provision, serves God's purposes (in judgment or salvation), and is filled with God's presence. From a biblical and Christian perspective, the most important "fact" about the created universe is its God relatedness.

So when we honor creation as "sacred," we do not imply that it is "divine." Treating the creation as if it or parts of it were "god" is idolatry. We are explicitly forbidden to worship anything within creation (Deut. 4:15–20; cf. Job 31:26–28). Indeed, it is of the essence of human idolatry, our truly original sin, that we exchanged worship of and gratitude to the one, true living God for the worship of elements of creation itself—with disastrous consequences (Rom. 1:18–32). No, by the sacredness of creation, we mean its God relatedness. Creation is good *in relation to* the good God who created it, and therefore our attitudes and actions within creation reflect our response to its Creator and our God.

Creation Is Good in Relation to Human Beings

So it is God's earth because he made it. But it is also our earth. "The highest heavens belong to the LORD, but the earth he has given to the children of Adam" (Ps. 115:16 AT). The earth is the place of human habitation. It remains under God's ownership, but it is also placed under human responsibility. The earth is, in some sense, "given" to human beings in a way that it is not said to be "given" to other animals.

Now at one level, of course, we are indeed animals among the animals, creatures among the creatures. But in what sense are we different? What makes the human species special or unique? At first sight, the Bible stresses much more what we have in common with the rest of the animals created by God than anything different or superior.

- Both animals and humans are blessed and instructed to multiply (Gen. 1:22, 28).

- Both humans and land creatures are created on the "sixth day" (vv. 24–31).
- The earth itself "brings forth" living creatures (v. 24), while humans are formed "from the dust of the ground" (2:7)—hardly a mark of our superiority!
- Humans enjoy "the breath of life," but so do all the other living creatures that breathe (1:30; 6:17; 7:15, 22; cf. Ps. 104:29–30).
- The same Hebrew phrase that describes the man in Genesis 2:7, "living being," is used of marine life in 1:20–21 (translated "living creatures," "living thing") and of "every living creature on earth" in 9:10.
- God provides both animals and humans with food (1:29–30).

It is a matter of wonder and rejoicing that we share with all the other animals in the love, care, and provision of God (Ps. 104:14–30). We are 'adam (human) from the 'adamah (ground).[5] We are creatures of the Creator God, and that is wonderful! To acknowledge that we are God's creatures like all the rest is not to demean our humanity but, rather, to celebrate the incredible capacity and power of the God who brought this whole magnificent biosphere into existence—including us.

What, then, makes us different from all the other species on the planet? Two things are affirmed in Genesis: first, that we are created in the image of God in order to be equipped to exercise dominion within creation (Gen. 1:26–28), and second, that we are placed on the earth (initially in the garden in Eden) in order to serve and care for it (Gen. 2:15). We are created to rule and located to serve.

CREATED TO RULE (GEN. 1:26–28)

> Then God said, "Let us make mankind in our image, in our likeness, so that they may rule over the fish in the sea

5. The word human comes from the Latin humus—earth, soil. We are "earth creatures."

and the birds in the sky, over the livestock and all the wild
animals, and over all the creatures that move along the
ground."

> So God created mankind in his own image,
>   in the image of God he created them;
>   male and female he created them.

God blessed them and said to them, "Be fruitful and
increase in number; fill the earth and subdue it. Rule over the
fish in the sea and the birds in the sky and over every living
creature that moves on the ground." (Gen. 1:26–28)

The grammar of these familiar verses implies (as the NIV correctly
translates) that God created human beings *with the intention that*
they should exercise rule over the rest of the animal creation and
that he created us in the image of God *in order to equip us* for that
function. The two things (the image of God and dominion over creation) are not identical with each other, but they are closely related:
the first enables the second.

"Rule over" implies the kind of rule exercised by kings. We are
created to exercise the delegated kingship of God within creation.
Just as emperors set up statues (images) of themselves in the countries
they ruled to indicate their authority over those realms, so human
beings, as the image of God, represent the authority of the real King
of all creation.

But how does God exercise God's own kingship within creation?
The Psalms tell us. Psalm 145, which is addressed to "my God the
King," tells us that God exercises his kingship by being gracious,
good, compassionate, faithful, generous, protective, just, and loving
toward all he has made (see especially vv. 9, 13, 16, 17). Psalm 104
colors in the details. Those are the marks of God the King, including
the manner of his kingship over his nonhuman creation. Therefore,
if human beings are the image of *this* God, then human rule in creation was never a license to dominate, abuse, crush, waste, or destroy.
Those are the marks of *tyranny* manifesting itself in fallen human
arrogance, not *kingship* modeled on God's character and behavior.
We are to exercise kingship in creation in a way that reflects the God
who made us in his own image.

The ideal and true model of human kingship is expressed in 1 Kings 12:7. There the elders of Judah respond to the young King Rehoboam, who had just asked their advice as to how he should respond to the northern tribes' request that he lighten the load of oppression that Solomon had imposed on them. "They replied, 'If today you will be a servant to these people and serve them and give them a favorable answer, they will always be your servants.'" I do not think this was a cynical piece of realpolitik—meaning, "Give them a sop of favor today, and they'll be your slaves for life." Rather, I think it expresses God's desire for the relationship between rulers and the ruled, between governments and those being governed: mutual servanthood. That was the ideal. The people would serve the king—provided the king would serve them without injustice. Likewise, on this model of human kingship in creation, the earth will serve our needs—provided we exercise our kingship as God's image and in God's way, by serving and caring for it.

That leads us naturally to the second dimension of our distinctive human role. Not only are we created to rule as kings in the image of God; we are also located to serve as "priests" in the service of creation.

LOCATED TO SERVE (GEN. 2:15)

"The LORD God took the man and put him in the garden to serve it and to keep it" (Gen. 2:15 AT). What we see here, in this complementary text, is that human rule *over* creation (in Gen. 1) is to be exercised by human servanthood *for* creation (in Gen. 2). The pattern of servant-kingship is very clear, and it is modeled perfectly, of course, by Jesus himself—the perfect human being—when he deliberately demonstrates his status as Lord and Master by washing the disciples' feet. Kingship exercised in servanthood—that is God's intention for humanity, modeled by his own incarnate Son.

But the language of "serving and keeping" has another resonance. It is the language of priesthood. Repeatedly in Leviticus it is said that the task of the priests and Levites was to serve God in the tabernacle/temple and to keep all that God had entrusted to them there. Human beings have, then, a priestly role as well as a kingly role within creation—which is very significant in view of how God later speaks of the role of Israel among the nations (as a "kingdom of priests"; Exod. 19:6) and how Revelation describes the role of redeemed humanity within the new creation: "You have made them to be a kingdom and priests to serve our God, and they will reign on the earth" (Rev. 5:10).[6]

The language of God placing his image within creation has temple overtones as well, for that is where the images of the gods were indeed placed—in their temples. With the cosmos functioning as the macro-temple of its Creator, God places his own image—the living human being—in his temple to dwell with him there. Creation functions as the dwelling place of God, and human beings function as the image of God, ruling and serving creation on his behalf.

The Glory of Creation[7]

So far in this chapter we have been "looking back," in a sense, to the goodness of God's creation as it came from God's hand—or rather,

6. Jonathan Leeman, in presenting his biblical understanding of mission, traces in Scripture two story lines in relation to the kingly and priestly roles of humanity and also of God's people, the church in mission. The first is "Ruling as Sons—A Kingly Storyline," which "suggests that the church possesses a broad mission: to image God in everything; to live as just and righteous dominion-enjoying sons of the king." I agree, which is why I interpret the fifth mark of mission as "creation care" not merely in the narrowly environmental sense but in the sense of all the ways in which we human beings live and work responsibly in the everyday routines of life in God's created world. And then the second story line is "Mediating God's Judgments—A Priestly Storyline," in which "God has authorized churches to mediate his judgments in the declaration of salvation and in the separation of a people unto himself in spite of all their sin and rebellion. Narrowly speaking, then, the mission of the church, in some sense of the word, is to make disciples by declaring or mediating God's judgments, which it does through gospel proclamation, baptism and the Lord's Supper, and instruction." Jonathan Leeman, "Soteriological Mission: Focusing in on the Mission of Redemption," in *Four Views on the Church's Mission*, ed. Jason S. Sexton, Counterpoints: Bible and Theology (Grand Rapids: Zondervan, 2017), 23–29, here 26, 29.

7. Parts of this section and the next are adapted from a chapter I wrote for a symposium on creation care: "The Care of Creation, the Gospel and Our Mission," in *Creation Care in Christian Mission*, ed. Kapya J. Kaoma, Regnum Edinburgh Centenary Series 29 (Oxford: Regnum Books International, 2015), 184–97. 978-1-908355-94-2. Used by permission.

arose from God's word. God repeatedly declared his created works to be "good," and we have explored some dimensions of what that means in relation to God and to human beings made in God's image. Now it is time to "look around," at the creation as we now experience it. For even though we know that we live as fallen sinners on the earth that lies under God's curse (since Genesis 3 and act 2 of the great story), nevertheless we are surrounded by the creation that still reveals the glory of its Creator. The Bible often connects the glory of God to what it says about creation. We can see this connection in two ways: God's glory is expressed through the *praise* of creation, and God's glory is seen in the *fullness* of creation.

God's Glory Expressed through the Praise of Creation

When I was a child growing up in a Presbyterian church in Belfast, I had to learn the Westminster Shorter Catechism of the Westminster Confession of Faith. The first question I was drilled to answer was, "What is the chief end of man?"—by which was meant, What is the ultimate purpose and goal of humanity's existence? The prescribed answer is "Man's chief end is to glorify God, and to enjoy him forever."[8] I believe the same question and the same answer could be applied to creation as a whole, not just to human beings. Creation exists for the praise and glory of God, for God's enjoyment of his creation, and for its enjoyment of him.

If that is so, then it means that the ultimate purpose of human life (to glorify God and enjoy him) is not something that *distinguishes* us from the rest of creation but something we *share in common* with the rest of creation.

It is obvious that human beings glorify God in uniquely human ways, with our rationality, language, emotions, poetry, music, art, technical skills, inventiveness, and so on—"hearts and hands and minds and voices, in our choicest psalmody," as the hymn says.[9] We know what it is *for us as human beings* to praise and glorify God.

---

8. The Westminster Shorter Catechism, in *The Creeds of Christendom*, vol. 3, *The Evangelical Protestant Creeds*, ed. Philip Schaff, 6th ed. (1931; repr., Grand Rapids: Baker, 1990), 676.

9. From Francis Pott's hymn "Angel Voices Ever Singing" (1861).

But the Bible affirms that *all creation* already praises God and can be summoned repeatedly to do so.

> All your works praise you, LORD;
> > your faithful people extol you. (Ps. 145:10)

> My mouth will speak in praise of the LORD.
> > Let every creature praise his holy name
> > for ever and ever. (Ps. 145:21)

> Praise the LORD from the earth,
> > you great sea creatures and all ocean depths,
> lightning and hail, snow and clouds,
> > stormy winds that do his bidding,
> you mountains and all hills,
> > fruit trees and all cedars,
> wild animals and all cattle,
> > small creatures and flying birds,
> kings of the earth and all nations,
> > you princes and all rulers on earth,
> young men and women,
> > old men and children.

> Let them praise the name of the LORD,
> > for his name alone is exalted. (Ps. 148:7–13)

And there are hints not only that creation praises God but that God takes delight and joy in—and even has fun with—his creation. That great psalm of creation, Psalm 104, not only celebrates the existence of the great sea creatures (nicknamed "Leviathan") but may actually portray God himself playing with them in the ocean.

> There is the sea, vast and spacious,
> > teeming with creatures beyond number—
> > living things both large and small.
> There the ships go to and fro,
> > and Leviathan, which you formed *to frolic there*. (Ps. 104:25–26)

That last verb can very legitimately be translated "whom you formed to play with" (as the ESV footnote offers). The poetic imagination that can picture Yahweh God in all kinds of anthropomorphic actions and emotions invites us to imagine him joyfully splashing around with whales in the ocean. And why not?

After all, the psalmists can also picture trees singing and rivers clapping their hands—the whole creation, heavens, earth, and sea, all rejoicing with jubilant songs of joy. Why? Because God is coming to put things right for humankind *and nature* together.

> Let all creation rejoice before the LORD, for he comes,
>   he comes to judge the earth.
> He will judge the world in righteousness
>   and the peoples in his faithfulness. (Ps. 96:13)

And that is the eschatological climax of the whole Bible story, a climax that explicitly includes the nonhuman creation; redeemed people from every human tribe, nation, and language; and the countless hosts of angels. John's vision reaches its fullest crescendo of praise when he says,

> Then I heard *every creature* in heaven and on earth and under the earth and on the sea, and all that is in them, saying:
>
> "To him who sits on the throne and to the Lamb
>   be praise and honor and glory and power,
>   for ever and ever!" (Rev. 5:13)

Now we may not be able to grasp or explain how creation praises God. Nor can we imagine how God receives the praise of his nonhuman creatures. Most simply, all God's creatures—animate and inanimate—praise and glorify God simply by being and doing what they were created for, and God is pleased and glorified when they do. The nonhuman creation brings glory to God simply by existing, for it exists only by God's sustaining and renewing power and thereby bears witness to God's greatness. The very fact that the creation is simply "there" is a glorifying tribute to the Creator himself, just as the sheer existence of Rembrandt's paintings glorifies Rembrandt. So just because we cannot define *how* creation praises and glorifies God, we should not deny what the Bible so often affirms—namely, that it *does*! The glory of creation consists in the fact that, in some way known fully only to God, it embodies and expresses the glory of God in its speechless voice of praise (Ps. 19:1–4).

God's Glory Seen in the Fullness of Creation

The glory of God is sometimes linked to the fullness of the earth. In Hebrew the phrase is literally "the filling of the earth." It is well observed that the creation account in Genesis 1 moves from functionless and *empty* to ordered and *full*. The great expanses—the sky, the oceans, the land—are successively populated with creatures that are blessed and instructed to "fill" the spaces assigned to them. The rich abundance of earth's biodiversity both arises from God's express intention and receives his repeated approval. God loves fullness, abundance, teeming diversity, growth, and multiplication!

Here are some more examples:

- Psalm 24:1: "To the LORD belongs the earth *and its fullness*."[10]
- Psalm 50:12: "To me belongs the world *and its fullness*" (after listing animals of the forest, cattle, birds, and insects).
- Psalm 104:31: "May the glory of the LORD endure forever; may the LORD rejoice in *his works*" (after celebrating the diversity of creatures, the psalmist places the glory of God in parallelism with "his works"—which is another way of expressing the fullness of creation, the amazing biodiversity of our planet).

This gives an interesting perspective on the cry of the seraphim during Isaiah's vision of God in the temple in Isaiah 6. What they cry out is literally "Holy, holy, holy—Yahweh *Tseva'ot*. The fullness [or "filling"] of all the earth—his glory" (Isa. 6:3 AT). The two dashes indicate the absence of any verb in the Hebrew sentence. This is a common feature of Hebrew that normally means that, in English translation, we insert an appropriate form of the verb "to be"

---

10. Here and in the following example, I prefer this more literal rendering of the Hebrew over the NIV's "everything in it."

somewhere. Accordingly, most translations render the second half as "the whole earth *is* full of his glory." Now that is true, of course! But reading the sentence in English in that way can diminish the weight of the word "full," as if the earth were merely a kind of receptacle that has been filled up with God's glory.

But the word "fullness" ("filling") stands emphatically first in the second half of the verse as a noun. It is "the fullness" that stands in apposition to "his glory," not simply the earth itself. And the fullness of the earth, as we have seen, is a shorthand expression for the abundance of life on earth in all its wonderful forms. Accordingly, it would be possible (as Young's Literal Translation does), to insert the word "is" into the sentence in this way: "The fullness of all the earth [is] his glory," meaning that the abundance and diversity of life that fills the earth constitutes the glory of God. That is to say, the glory of God is rendered to us in the overflowing plenitude of God's own creation.

Now, of course, we need to be careful not to read pantheism into such a statement. This is not suggesting that there is nothing more to God and his glory than the sum of creation itself. No, clearly God's glory as Creator *transcends* creation itself ("You have set your glory above the heavens" is a way that several psalms express that truth). But, having said that, we can certainly affirm that the glory of God is mediated to us through creation, not only in the awesome majesty of the heavens (Ps. 19:1), but also through the abundance of life on earth.

We live in a *glory-filled earth*, an earth that by its very abundance renders glory to God and reveals God's glory to us. And that is one reason why Paul says that people are without excuse when they fail to glorify God and give thanks to him (Rom. 1:20–21).

Creation Care and Mission

What does all this have to do with our main theme—mission? How does it help us answer the question of whether it is legitimate to include our responsible use of and care for creation within our theology and practice of mission? I would make two points, by way of conclusion, in response to that question.

First, in exercising care for God's creation, we are reflecting both the compassion and the justice of God. In other words, there is a sense in which creation care itself is an extension (a legitimate one, in my view) of the third and fourth marks of mission, exercised not only toward fellow human beings but toward the nonhuman creation.

We are reflecting God's *compassion* because caring for God's creation is essentially an unselfish form of love, exercised for the sake of creatures who cannot thank or repay you. It is a form of truly biblical and godly altruism. In this respect, it reflects the same quality in the love of God—not only in the sense that God loves human beings despite our unlovable enmity toward him, but also in the wider sense that "the Lord . . . has compassion on [or is loving toward] *all he has made*" (Ps. 145:9; cf. vv. 13, 17). Again, Jesus could use God's loving care for birds and adornment of grasses and flowers as a model for his even greater love for his human children. If God cares with such minute compassion for his nonhuman creation, then surely so should those who wish to emulate him.

We are reflecting God's *justice* because environmental action is a form of defending the weak against the strong, the defenseless against the powerful, the violated against the attacker, the voiceless against the stridency of the greedy. And these, too, are features of the character of God as expressed in his exercise of justice. Psalm 145 includes God's provision for all his creatures in its definition of his *righteousness* as well as his love (Ps. 145:13–17). In fact, that psalm places God's care for creation in precise parallel with his liberating and vindicating acts of justice for his people—thus bringing the creational and redemptive traditions of the Old Testament together in beautiful harmony.

So it is not surprising, then, that when the Old Testament identifies the marks of a righteous *person* (whose righteousness is, of course, a reflection of *God's*), it does not stop at their practical concern for poor and needy *humans* (though that is, of course, the dominant note). It is true that "the righteous care about justice for the poor" (Prov. 29:7). But the sage also makes the warmhearted observation that "the righteous care for the needs of their *animals*" (Prov. 12:10). Biblical mission is as holistic as biblical righteousness.

Second, when we care for creation, our care is an extension of another biblical principle: namely, that our treatment of other humans is an "embodiment" or expression of our treatment of God. The Wisdom literature articulates this principle in relation to God as our Creator.

Whoever oppresses the poor shows contempt for their Maker,
but whoever is kind to the needy honors God. (Prov. 14:31)

Whoever mocks the poor shows contempt for their Maker. (Prov. 17:5)

Whoever is kind to the poor lends to the LORD. (Prov. 19:17)

The principle is that, since all human beings are made in God's image, whatever we do to other *people* (for good or ill), we are doing to *God*. This is the principle that Jesus extended in relation to himself in Matthew 25.

No precise biblical verse that I know of applies this principle to the nonhuman creation, although Proverbs may be getting close when it affirms that "the righteous care for the needs of their animals, but the kindest acts of the wicked are cruel" (Prov. 12:10)—given that righteousness and kindness reflect the character and will of God. Nevertheless, it does seem to me that there is a legitimate extension of this same principle. Since the fullness of created life on earth in some sense constitutes or communicates God's glory, then whatever we do on the earth that in some way fulfills the mandates of Genesis 1 and 2—by developing, enhancing, and properly using the resources of the earth while at the same time serving and caring for it—*acknowledges and contributes to the glory of God*. We glorify God when we treat with godly respect and care that which itself glorifies God.

Conversely, the negative implication is that whatever needlessly destroys, degrades, pollutes, and wastes the life of the earth and thereby diminishes the fullness of the earth in its biblical sense *diminishes God's glory*. And that is surely a serious matter. That is one part of what is at stake, from a biblical, Christian point of view, in the attitudes, positions, and actions we take in the current ecological crisis and debate.

How we treat the earth reflects how we treat its Creator—and ours.

The goodness and glory of creation are inextricably connected with the goodness and glory of God. It is hard to see, then, how any understanding of mission that longs to share God's goodness and promote God's glory could exclude God's creation from the full range of its concerns and engagement.

8

The Goal of Creation

Let's recall our purpose in this book. We are seeking to express the relationship between the great story and the Great Commission, exploring a missional hermeneutic that is grounded in reading the Bible as one whole narrative that renders to us the mission of God and summons us to play our part in it. In our last chapter, we viewed creation in the light of act 1 of the biblical narrative. Now we turn to act 7, the other end of the story. We are no longer just looking *back* to the original creation and its intrinsic, God-affirmed goodness. Nor are we only looking *around* at the glory of God expressed in the praise of creation and the fullness of the earth. Now we are looking *forward* to God's ultimate purpose for creation. And it is a very encouraging direction to look! What is creation's eschatological goal and destiny? And how does the combination of the beginning and ending of the biblical story of creation impact our missional understanding and practice?

God's Redemptive Purpose Includes Creation

The first thing we have to say is that creation *needs* redemption. The movement of the biblical drama from act 1 (creation) to act 2 (rebellion) impacted more than the human race alone. The Bible makes it

128

very clear that sin and evil have affected the natural order as well as human life. We touched on this in chapter 2 above, but we need to bring it into sharper focus here.

"Cursed is the ground because of you," said God to Adam (Gen. 3:17). The Hebrew word translated "the ground" (NIV) in this verse (and sometimes "the earth" elsewhere) is *'adamah*, not the much more common *'erets*. Both words have a broad range of meaning, and we can't sharply differentiate them. Nevertheless, *'adamah* here most likely refers to the ground as "soil"[1]—that is, the earth as the dry-land space for human habitation, what we live on and live off. It probably does not refer here to the whole earth as a biosphere of land, sea, and sky—the whole planet (in our sense).

I interpret the curse on the ground, therefore, as primarily referring to human life and work on the ground, especially work to produce food (as the words of God immediately suggest)—this includes farming, naturally, but also all forms of human work that are essential to feeding ourselves—rather than referring to the geological structures and the functioning of the planet (as we now know them). That is, I do not personally believe that we should attribute all natural phenomena that are potentially destructive (the shifting of tectonic plates, earthquakes, tsunamis, volcanic eruptions, etc.) to "the curse." Those geological realities are simply part of the way God has made life on planet earth possible at all. For without the shifting of tectonic plates there would be no mountains, no rivers, no soil, no climatic variation, no precipitation, nor many other features of the earth that make it fit for organic life and ultimately human habitation. We might be inclined to wonder why God arranged the cosmic, geological, and biological "natural history" of our planet to require these mechanisms and processes that are essential to organic life and human existence as a species, but we might also find ourselves hesitating to dictate to God that he should have thought of a better way to design a home for us (and for himself).

Nevertheless, in that remarkable chapter 8 of Romans, Paul does make the clear theological affirmation that *the whole of creation* is

---

1. The word is etymologically linked to *'adam*—the earth creature, the one from the soil. This is similar to the roots of the word *human* in the Latin *humus*, meaning "soil."

frustrated, subjected to futility in some sense, and that this is by God's will. It is hard to know exactly how Paul envisaged that "frustration," but given Paul's insistence that all creation (including humanity) exists to bring glory to God, it seems probable that he is implying that while creation continues to do that to some extent (as his Scriptures told him repeatedly), it is frustrated in the fullness of its glory-proclaiming task because of human sin and rebellion.[2] As long as the one species that was created in the image of God to be king and priest within creation is falling short of the glory of God (Rom. 3:23), creation itself, along with humanity, is in a state of "bondage to decay."

But—and here is the spectacular good news of the biblical gospel—creation was subjected by God "*in hope*" (Rom. 8:20). And, as we saw in chapter 2, the word *hope* in the Bible is not a weak and desperate longing that, just maybe, things might turn out better eventually. Rather, it is confident certainty grounded in the promises of God and the assurance generated by his mighty deeds already accomplished in acts 3 and 4 of the great drama of Scripture so far. And that hope—the substance of act 7 of the drama—is that "the creation itself will be liberated . . . and brought into the freedom and glory of the children of God" (Rom. 8:21; notice the word *glory* again, as well as the redemptive vocabulary *liberated* and *freedom*). That is the future God has for his creation.

The truth is, then, that just as creation shares in the effects of our sin, so we will share in the fullness of creation's redemption. Creation suffers with us and because of us. But we will rejoice with creation when God liberates it, along with us, from all suffering and death. We are not going to be saved *out of* the earth; rather, we will be saved *along with* the earth. For God's ultimate purpose is "to bring unity to all things in heaven and on earth under Christ" (Eph. 1:10—one of the most astonishingly universal and cosmic articulations of the mission of God in the Bible).

2. I have to add that when I am awestruck by some magnificent view in creation—of mountains in brilliant sunshine and scudding clouds, or the thundering vastness of the ocean beside towering cliffs, or the silent and majestic dignity of a centuries-old tree, or a spectacularly gorgeous sunrise or sunset—I think to myself, *If this is what creation can do when it's "frustrated," imagine what it will be like when it is "liberated"!*

In chapter 4 we observed how the phrases of Christ's Great Commission and the theological assumption behind them are deeply rooted in the Old Testament Scriptures. The same is true for Paul's affirmations about the future of creation. Paul did not invent the hope and vision he holds out. Rather, he sees that what God has accomplished through the Messiah Jesus in his cross and resurrection is the fulfillment of scriptural promises for *creation*, not just for humanity. God's promise to Abraham that *all nations* on earth would be blessed through him (a "mystery" as to how it could ever happen) is now revealed as being fulfilled "through the gospel . . . in Christ" (Eph. 3:6). Likewise, the promised restoration of *creation* will be accomplished by God through Christ (Col. 1:15–20).

The Scriptures must be fulfilled. And the Prophets certainly included creation in their understanding of God's salvation plans. Or, as we might say, they included ecology in their eschatology—none more so than Isaiah.

- The messianic era under the rule of a future son of David will inaugurate not only international justice and peace among the nations but also environmental harmony and freedom from predation and fear (Isa. 11:6–9).

- The reign of the king of righteousness and the outpouring of God's Spirit will bring justice, peace, and fruitfulness not just to people but to nature too (Isa. 32:1, 15–20).

- The restoration and return of the redeemed, when God comes, will be accompanied not only by miracles among humans but also by surging creational fertility and abundance (Isa. 35).

- God is already in the business of "creating" (the verb is participial, with a sense of something ongoing in the present and future) "new heavens and a new earth" (Isa. 65:17). The picture that follows those words depicts human life on that "new earth": it is full of joy and free from tears; it is life fulfilling and family building; there is deep satisfaction and fruitfulness in ordinary labor and freedom from the curses of frustration and injustice; *and also* it exhibits the reality of

environmental peace and harmony in the natural world (Isa.
65:17–25). It is a glorious picture that provided the images
and vocabulary for Revelation 21–22.

Such anticipation and glorious vision are not confined to the
Prophets. They find expression in the regular worship of Israel in
the Psalms. We have already noted the way some psalms celebrate
the *present* reality of creation benefiting from God's provision,
while bringing God praise, glory, and enjoyment. But when they
contemplate the full establishment of the reign of Yahweh, not
only is it something to be proclaimed among the *nations*, it is also
a cause for rejoicing and celebration by the whole *creation*, for God
is coming to judge the earth—to put all things right for creation
and the peoples.

> Say among the nations, "The LORD reigns."
> The world is firmly established, it cannot be moved;
> he will judge the peoples with equity.
>
> Let the heavens rejoice, let the earth be glad;
> let the sea resound, and all that is in it.
> Let the fields be jubilant, and everything in them;
> let all the trees of the forest sing for joy.
> Let all creation rejoice before the LORD, for he comes,
> he comes to judge the earth.
> He will judge the world in righteousness
> and the peoples in his faithfulness. (Ps. 96:10–13)

Now we might be tempted to treat all these Old Testament expectations for the created order as merely symbolic or metaphorical
in some way, referring only to God's plans for human salvation.
Or we might condescend to relativize them historically as "Old
Testament earthiness"—the more primitive, earthbound limita-
tion of living, believing, and hoping, as the Israelites did, only
in the context of the physical world of their present experience.
This limited, earthly perspective is then transcended, it would be
alleged, by the more spiritual message of the New Testament that
transports us and our expectations up from this material earth to

our real spiritual and heavenly environment. Not at all. That kind of Platonic dualism simply won't do, either in the Old Testament or in the New.

Paul speaks of a new, liberated *creation* being brought to birth within the womb of *this* creation, whose groanings are the labor pains of creation's future as well as our own. That is his wonderfully suggestive portrayal of the present and future in Romans 8:18–25. And it is thoroughly physical. For we who "wait eagerly for . . . the redemption of our bodies" (v. 23) will inhabit the new creation in our resurrection bodies, modeled on the prototype resurrection body of Jesus, "who, by the power that enables him to bring everything under his control, will transform our lowly bodies so that they will be like his glorious body" (Phil. 3:21; cf. 1 John 3:2). It is vital that we grasp the integrated link that Paul makes in Romans 8 between the *resurrection of the body* and the *liberation of all creation* from its bondage to decay. Our human future is bound up with creation's future—and vice versa. Our future is not an *escape* from a doomed creation but the enjoyment of a liberated creation—a creation that, presently and reciprocally, longs for the redemption of our bodies for that very prospect.

That is one reason why the bodily resurrection of Jesus is so vitally important. The disciples, in their shock and fear, imagine that the risen Jesus is a ghost, but he deliberately demonstrates to his disciples that he is fully physical—with body parts, flesh and bones, and the ability to be touched, to eat food, to light a fire and make breakfast (Luke 24:37–43; John 21). And yet, of course, in his resurrection body, he has capacities and powers that transcend the normal limitations of space and time. In other words, the risen Jesus is the prototype of what Paul calls "the spiritual body" (1 Cor. 15:44), which is not somehow spiritual in the sense of nonphysical; rather, it is supraphysical, already part of the new creation in all its eschatological physicality.

The resurrection of Jesus of Nazareth, then, is God's "Yes!" to the whole physical, created order. The risen Jesus is the firstborn of the new creation. And we shall be like him—fully and bodily human, inhabiting the new, renewed, and unified heaven and earth, the new creation.

Creation Is Destined for Purging and Renewal, Not Obliteration

At this point we need to address a question that is often raised in relation to the future of creation. What is meant by the language of fiery destruction and cosmic conflagration that we find in 2 Peter 3?

> But the day of the Lord will come like a thief. The heavens will disappear with a roar; the elements will be destroyed by fire, and the earth and everything done in it will be laid bare.
>
> Since everything will be destroyed in this way, what kind of people ought you to be? You ought to live holy and godly lives as you look forward to the day of God and speed its coming. That day will bring about the destruction of the heavens by fire, and the elements will melt in the heat. But in keeping with his promise we are looking forward to a new heaven and a new earth, where righteousness dwells. (2 Pet. 3:10–13)

Surely, some people argue, the picture of the day of the Lord given here portrays final *destruction*, not redemption and renewal. They assume a radical discontinuity between this creation and whatever lies ahead when Christ returns. This creation, they envision, is destined for obliteration through cosmic incineration.[3]

However, we need to see the context and argument of the whole chapter. Peter is arguing against those who scoff at the idea of a future judgment, complacently believing that everything will go on, just as it always has, forever (vv. 3–4). What they forget, says Peter, is that such an attitude was around before the flood, but God *did* intervene

---

3. This way of thinking sometimes goes along with a dismissive attitude toward the whole concept of creation care. "If the earth is going to be burned up, why should I bother caring for it now?" My answer to this is threefold: First, as explained below, I do not think that is what Peter is saying. Second, *even if* the earth (the whole cosmos, heaven and earth, says Peter) will end in (literal) fire, this is no more reason for refusing to care for it *now* than the prospect that our earthly bodies may end up in a crematorium is a reason for not caring for *them* now. Imagine the doctor who says to a patient who is anxious about some serious illness: "Well, you're going to die anyway, so why should I care for you now?" Both the earth and our earthly bodies are God's good creation entrusted to our care and stewardship. Third, the sacredness of creation and of human bodies rests further on the Bible's affirmation of both the resurrection of the body and the redeemed heaven and earth—a combination of truths that Paul explicitly makes in Romans 8.

and act in judgment. So God will assuredly and finally do again in the future what he prefigured in the past. What he did *then* by water, he will do *in the end* by fire.

Now the key thing to observe here is that the language of the world's "destruction" is used of both events. Look at the parallel points in verses 6–7: "By these waters also the world of that time was deluged and *destroyed*. By the same word the present heavens and earth are reserved for fire, being kept for the day of judgment and *destruction* of the ungodly" (2 Pet. 3:6–7).

What was destroyed in the flood? Not the whole planet or creation itself but the ungodly human society on the earth at that time— the "destruction of the ungodly," as Peter says. So the apocalyptic language of fire in the second part of the chapter, then, should be understood in its biblical sense of purging, cleansing judgment, just as the language of water is used in the first part of the chapter.

Creation will be purged, swept clean of all evil, and "the earth and everything done in it will be laid bare"—laid bare, that is, to the all-seeing eyes of our Creator and Judge. This is an image of inescapable *judgment*, not one of total obliteration. It portrays the fiery cleansing of the earth, the destruction of "the world" in the sense of the world that stands in sinful rebellion against God. And what comes next? Peter continues with that wonderful verse 13: "But in keeping with his promise we are looking forward to a new heaven and a new earth, where righteousness dwells." This speaks of a renewed, cleansed, restored cosmos, a unified heaven and earth that will be the home no longer of rebellion and ungodliness but of righteousness, for God will dwell there with his people.

We might put it like this: If we relate 2 Peter 3 to our outline of the great story as the drama of Scripture, then verses 10–12 portray act 6 (the final judgment, which will include the cleansing of all creation in its scope), whereas verse 13 points to act 7 (the new creation, so much more fully portrayed in Rev. 21–22).

To stay with the imagery for a moment: the language of verse 10 certainly calls to mind a terrifying cosmic furnace. But it is not an incinerating furnace in which nothing is left but useless ash. Rather, it is a smelting furnace in which all the unwanted dross is consumed, and what emerges is the pure gold of God's new creation. The future of God's creation is one not of obliteration and evacuation to somewhere else but of cleansing, restoration, and eternal righteousness.

But how will all this be accomplished? In fact, it already has been! We may not be able to imagine with our finite brains what the new creation will be like or how God will do it, just as we cannot conceptualize the resurrection of our bodies, when so many bodies of believers have long since dissolved in the earth, in the sea, or in the fires or bellies of beasts in martyrdom. But Paul assures us that both the resurrection of our bodies and the redemption of creation are already guaranteed, accomplished in anticipation, through the cross and resurrection of Jesus Christ.

Creation Has Been Reconciled to God through the Cross of Christ

Colossians 1:15–20 must be one of the most breathtaking passages Paul ever wrote about Jesus Christ.

> The Son is the image of the invisible God, the firstborn over all creation. For in him all things were created: things in heaven and on earth, visible and invisible, whether thrones or powers or rulers or authorities; all things have been created through him and for him. He is before all things, and in him all things hold together. And he is the head of the body, the church; he is the beginning and the firstborn from among the dead, so that in everything he might have the supremacy. For God was pleased to have all his fullness dwell in him, and through him to reconcile to himself all things, whether things on earth or things in heaven, by making peace through his blood, shed on the cross.

Paul paints in truly cosmic colors and dimensions here. Five times he uses the phrase "all things" (*ta panta*), and by adding the words "in heaven and on earth," Paul makes it clear that he means the whole of creation at every possible level. And he tells us that the whole creation

- was created by Christ and for Christ;
- is sustained in existence by Christ; and

- *has been reconciled to God by Christ*—specifically "by making peace through his blood, shed on the cross" (v. 20).

That last phrase is vitally important. We must "lift up our eyes" and see the truly cosmic, creational scope of Christ's death. Paul says that through the cross God has accomplished the reconciliation of all creation. This must be what Paul has in mind when he summarizes the whole plan of God to unify all creation in and under Christ (Eph. 1:10).

It is fascinating to see how Paul immediately continues. "*And you also*," he starts verse 21 (cf. ESV). "You" (plural) is emphatic at the start of the sentence. In the vast creation-wide, Christ-centered, church-forming context of verses 15–20, Paul turns to his gentile readers to assure them that, amazingly, they have a place in this grand plan of God through their faith in this gospel—using exactly the same word about *them*, "reconciled" (v. 22), that he had just used about *creation* (v. 20)—and by the same means, Christ's death. God's big story has become their story—as gentiles and as individual persons.

We tend to present the gospel the other way around. We start at the personal level: "Christ died to atone for your sins and give you eternal life." Wonderfully true; praise God! Then we might go on to the ecclesial level: "All of us who are redeemed by Christ are part of the church, the people of God, the body of Christ, so you need to join a church." And just possibly we might go on to the rest of creation: "We have to live and work here on this earth until we die and go to heaven, or until Christ returns to take us home." We prioritize the individual and move (sometimes, eventually) to the big picture (or a deficient understanding of it).

In this text Paul moves in the exact opposite direction. He starts with the big story—Christ's cosmic lordship over all creation (which, as we saw in chapter 4, is where Jesus himself also starts in the so-called Great Commission; Matt. 28:18). Then he moves on to speak about the church, of which Christ is the head. Then he returns to the redemption of all creation through the cross. Only then does he come to individual believers who have heard the gospel and responded in faith. "You believers in Colossae," he says, "you also get to be part of this great story of cosmic creation and reconciliation by virtue of believing 'this gospel'—this good news for all creation. God has reconciled *you, too*, through the cross." This, then, is the gospel, the biblical gospel that includes all creation within the redeeming, saving, reconciling plan of God accomplished through the death and resurrection of Christ.

So to claim to be a Christian, to be a follower and disciple of Jesus, to be submitting to Jesus as Lord and King (which is surely definitional of what it means to be a Christian), and yet to have no concern about the creation, or even to reject with hostility those who do act on such concern, seems to me to be a denial of the biblical gospel, which proclaims that Jesus Christ is the Creator, Sustainer, and Redeemer of creation itself. I cannot claim Christ as *my* Lord and Savior while at the same time ignoring what the biblical gospel proclaims: he is *creation's* Lord and Reconciler.

What, then, is our final destination?

It is amazing (and regrettable) how many Christians believe that the world ends with us all leaving the earth behind and going off to heaven to live there instead. This broad assumption is doubtless due to the influence of countless hymns and songs that unfortunately use that kind of imagery—images of us going up, going home, soaring to realms above, going to our eternal rest, and so on. But that is decidedly not how the Bible ends. Check out act 7 again in chapter 2.

Now, of course, there is an important truth that gives great comfort and hope—that when believers die in faith and in Christ, they go to be with Christ. We are assured that they are safe, secure, and at rest, free from all the perils and sufferings of this earthly life. This is sometimes called "the intermediate state," meaning the passage of *earthly* time that we who remain experience between the moment of a believer's death and the return of Christ. The reality for the deceased believer is that he or she has, in a sense, left earthly time behind and entered into the new creational reality of the presence of the risen and ascended Christ. They are, in that defined sense, "in heaven." But the Bible makes it clear that the intermediate state is just that—*intermediate*. It is not our *final* destination merely to "go to heaven when we die."

The Bible's ultimate, dynamic movement in Revelation 21–22 is not up but down! That is, John does not see *us* all going up to heaven, but rather, he sees *God* coming down here, bringing the city of God, reunifying heaven and earth as his dwelling place with us, his bride, forever. Three times the loud voice from the throne of God says, *"with* humankind," *"with* them," *"with* them" (Rev. 21:3 AT). This is the glorious, ultimate fulfillment of the Immanuel sign. Remember, Immanuel does not mean "Us with God" but means "God with us." We do not go somewhere else to be with God; God comes to earth to be with us, just as the psalmists and prophets had prophesied and prayed for. "Oh, that you would rend the heavens and come down" (Isa. 64:1)! And God says, "I will!" And John says, "That's what I saw!"

Let's pull this all together. In the last chapter and in this one, we have sought to set creation itself within the missional hermeneutic of reading the Bible as one whole story. We have considered the goodness and glory of creation (reflecting act 1). And we have marveled at the goal of creation (acts 6 and 7) in the light of the redemptive, reconciling accomplishment of the cross and resurrection of Christ (act 4). What does all this mean, in a missional sense, for our ecological thinking and action in the here and now?

It means that in the godly use of and care for God's creation, we are doing two things at the same time. On the one hand, we are *exercising* the created role God gave us from the beginning as human beings made in God's image, ruling and serving as kings and priests within God's created order. In so doing we can properly be glorifying God in *all* our work within and for creation, including but not confined to work specifically related to the natural world ("creation care" as such: conservation, environmental biology, climate advocacy, and so on).

On the other hand, we are *anticipating* (in a prophetic sense) the role that we shall have in the new creation, when we shall fully assume our proper role of kings and priests, exercising the loving rule of God over the rest of his creation and serving it on God's behalf as the place of God's temple dwelling.

In other words, ecological action now is both a creational responsibility from the Bible's beginning and also an eschatological sign of the Bible's ending (which is, of course, a new beginning!). Christian ecological action points toward and anticipates the restoration of our proper human status and function in creation. It is to behave as we were originally created to behave—and as we shall one day be fully redeemed for.

The earth is waiting with eager longing for the revealing of its appointed kings and priests—that is, redeemed humanity glorifying God in the temple of his renewed, reconciled, and unified creation, under the lordship of Jesus Christ.

9

The Great Story,
the Great Commission,
and the Church's Mission

Let's review the journey we have taken. We have focused on one of the
ways in which the term *missional hermeneutic* is used—namely, by
reading the Bible as one vast narrative that renders to us the mission
of God. That "great story" is the context in which the Great Commission fits. The *story* tells us what *God* intends for his whole creation and all nations; the *commission* mandates *us* to be co-workers
with God under the lordship of Christ, in the certainty that God will
fulfill his intentions and achieve his mission.

When we begin to grasp the mission of God in its full biblical comprehensiveness, we must further ask how we should then construe the
corresponding mission of God's people. What constitutes the mission
of the church? Out of the many proposed answers to that question,
we have considered the so-called five marks of mission (evangelism,
teaching, compassion, justice, and creational responsibility) as a rea-
sonably comprehensive and biblically justified summary of the core
essentials of our missional obligations, as we respond in grateful
obedience to the prior grace and redemptive accomplishment of God

in Christ. Each of those five marks is rooted in Scripture, and all of them express in their various ways what it means to call Jesus Lord. I strove to emphasize that the centrality of the gospel of the kingdom of God—the reign of God in and through Christ as Lord—is what holds together every dimension of what has come to be known as "integral mission."

For the sake of simplicity, I combined those five marks into three focal areas of missional endeavor: building or growing the *church* through evangelism and teaching; serving *society* through works of compassion and advocacy for justice; and responsibly using, stewarding, and caring for *creation*. Those three areas occupied chapters 5–7.

In this concluding chapter, we must address the so-what question that any individual believer or church might find themselves asking. What implications for ourselves and our churches emerge from this survey of the great story, the Great Commission, and the contours of integral mission? How does such a missional hermeneutic shape not only our theology of mission but also our practice?

Three points seem to follow, and the first is the foundation for the others.

God's Whole Mission Is for God's Whole Church

One of the reasons we stressed the importance of the election of Abraham for a biblical theology of mission (in chap. 2) is because it combines two crucially important elements: (1) the ultimate intention of God to bring all nations within the sphere of his blessing (which Paul calls "the gospel" in Gal. 3:8) and (2) the means God chose to accomplish that intention—namely, a people, the seed of Abraham.[1] The foundational call and promise of God in Genesis 12:1–3 include

---

1. Ultimately, of course, "the means" by which the living, triune God has opened up the possibility of blessing for all nations is through the cross and resurrection of God the Son, Jesus of Nazareth, in the power of the Holy Spirit. But the point here is that the Jesus who died and rose again was (is) precisely the Messiah of Israel and that God created and chose Israel as the people through whom God himself would "take frail flesh and die" (from Samuel Crossman's hymn "My Song Is Love Unknown" [1664]).

both elements in its climactic last line: "and *all peoples* on earth will be blessed *through you*" (since "you" will become the great nation God had just promised in the previous verses). That promise is repeated four more times in Genesis (18:18–19; 22:18; 26:4–5, 28:14). And the link between God's *mission* and God's *people* is most clearly implied in Genesis 18:18–19. Having stated once more his intention to bless all nations (v. 18), God declares that the very reason he had chosen Abraham was in order to create a community that would walk in God's way, so that God could keep that promise (v. 19).[2]

So, from the start, the *existence* of the people of God on earth is bound up with the *mission* of God for all nations.[3] That's what I mean by the two "wholes" in the heading above.

Mission is not a specialist activity for a few professionals (missionaries or mission partners). *The church as a whole* exists for the sake of God's mission. As has been said, it is not so much that God has a mission for the church as that God has the church for his mission. God brought the church into existence (as the people in organic spiritual continuity with Abraham) because God is God of all creation and all nations and God is purposively at work in all history for the reconciliation and redemption of both. And God creates and calls his redeemed people to be co-workers with him in his redemptive mission in the course of earthly *history*, then to be his kings and priests and servants in the glorious, ongoing, purposeful life of the new creation for all *eternity*.

And that great cosmic truth underlies the opening claim of the crucified and risen Lord Jesus Christ and the immediately following imperatives in the Great Commission: "All authority in heaven and on earth has been given to me. Therefore go and make disciples of all nations" (Matt. 28:18–19). As I have said throughout, I am not

---

2. The intentionality I have built into that sentence is present in the Hebrew sentence as well, where the word *lema'an*, "in order that," occurs twice, connecting the three clauses of the sentence into one affirmation of divine purposefulness (Gen. 18:19).

3. I have explored all the ramifications of this simple statement in much greater depth in my books *The Mission of God: Unlocking the Bible's Grand Narrative* (Downers Grove, IL: IVP Academic, 2006) and *The Mission of God's People: A Biblical Theology of the Church's Mission*, Biblical Theology for Life (Grand Rapids: Zondervan, 2010).

holding up the Great Commission as the only or most important biblical text for the authority and content of the church's mission. But even regarding it as manifestly *one such key text*, it is surely addressed both to the eleven disciples who stood or knelt in the presence of the risen Christ on the day of his ascension and to all disciples of Christ who obey his command and receive the promise of his presence till the end of the age.[4] The Great Commission is not just for mission agencies and societies; it is for the whole church, every church, and all disciples of the Lord Jesus Christ. It is, in fact, a self-replicating command, since obeying everything Jesus had taught must include the commands within the Great Commission itself.[5]

The *whole* church is, in that sense, missional. Every local church is a missional church, or it is not really being a church at all. They may be a group of religious people meeting for mutual support, but if they do not perceive the missional nature of their very existence (i.e., what they are actually *there for* as a church), then they have simply lost the plot—the Bible's plot. Everything a church is and does should be connected in some way to the purpose of the church's existence as the people of God in the first place, which is to serve the mission of God in history for the ultimate glory of God for eternity.

At this point an objection is sometimes raised: "If everything is mission, nothing is mission."[6] Usually this expresses the fear that if everything a church does is *described* as "mission," then there will be no clear or special category left for evangelism or sending out missionaries.[7]

---

4. The assumption that the Great Commission is for *all* disciples of Jesus Christ through all generations matches the way Jesus's great high-priestly prayer in John 17 is prayed—not only for the disciples who were in the room with him at the time but "also for those who will believe in [Jesus] through their message" (John 17:20).

5. This is a point made by Craig L. Blomberg in "The Great Commission," in *Devotions on the Greek New Testament: 52 Reflections to Inspire and Instruct*, ed. J. Scott Duvall and Verlyn D. Verbrugge (Grand Rapids: Zondervan, 2010), 25–26.

6. I believe this oft-repeated tag originated with Bishop Stephen Neill.

7. I have always found this to be a rather meaningless and misleading slogan, since it confuses different senses, or referents, of the word *mission*. To illustrate its superficiality: We could insist that, biblically, *every aspect of a Christian's life and a church's work is a form of ministry*—i.e., the service of God. But suppose that someone, protective of ordained pastoral ministry and fearing it might be disregarded, retorted to that affirmation in italics with the slogan "If everything is ministry, nothing

Sadly, there are indeed some churches that call themselves "missional" but seem to have given up on cross-cultural, international mission and church planting, and even on any explicit evangelistic outreach at all. They use the term "missional" to mean little more than their church's hopefully beneficial servant presence in their local community (which is a good thing in itself, of course). In contrast to that, I hope it is clear from what I have written in chapter 4, about the centrality of the gospel and the nonnegotiable necessity of bearing verbal witness to what God has done in Christ, that I am utterly committed to the importance of evangelism and church planting, nationally and internationally. But evangelism and church planting simply are not the *whole* of what I believe the Bible includes in the mission of the church, in the sense of all that God has called the church into existence for. The whole church is called to participate in the whole mission of God. And every aspect and dimension of a church's life should be contributing in one way or another to motivating and equipping us for our fundamental raison d'être, which is to participate in the mission of God in the world.

I have elsewhere put this as follows:

> In this regard, Lesslie Newbigin made a very helpful distinction between missional *dimension* and missional *intention* in the life of the church. Because the church exists for the sake of God's mission, its whole life (worship, fellowship, pastoring, teaching, outreach, etc.) has a missional dimension, simply because that is why and how the church is meant to be. Everything the church is and does should be connected in some way to our very reason for existence as the people of God in the first place, which is to serve the mission of God for the ultimate glory of God. Church activities should be evaluated in terms of what the church exists for. Are they, as we say, "fit for purpose"? That is the missional *dimension* of all church life.
>
> But the church also acts with missional *intention*. It engages in specific actions and initiatives that are planned, resourced, and carried

---

is ministry." Or, similarly, suppose someone thought that the affirmation that *the whole of a Christian's life and work should, biblically, be seen as a form of worship offered in gratitude to God* would lead to the abandonment of specific ecclesial acts of corporate worship, warning, "If everything is worship, nothing is worship." I think we can see the shallow confusion in that kind of dismissive rhetoric.

out with deliberate intention of bearing witness, in word and deed, to the good news of the kingdom of God and fulfilling the broad range of commitments found in the Great Commission and expounded through the whole Bible story. These are summarized, but certainly not exhausted, by those "five marks of mission."[8]

So, then, God's whole mission is for God's whole church. *But everybody can't do everything!* We need not be overwhelmed. Sometimes people say to me, after a sermon or lecture about integral mission along the lines of chapter 4, "You talk about all these different kinds of mission, like preaching the gospel, teaching theology, feeding the hungry, caring for creation, and so on, but there's only one of me. I can't do all that!" My reply is usually, "Yes, I see your point. I suspect God thought of that too, which is why he created the church." It takes the *whole* church, with *all* its members, to engage in God's whole mission. It is a case not of *everybody* doing *everything* but of everybody being intentional about *something*, according to the gifting and leading of God. In that way the whole church, in all its diversity, will be involved in multiple ways in participating in the mission of God.

So then, God's whole mission is for God's whole church. That leads to our second so-what response.

The Whole Church's Mission Includes Every Church Member

If the church as a whole exists for God's mission, then so do all its members. If the church is missional by definition, then all Christians are missional by calling. We need to radically challenge the mistaken paradigm that mission is something done only by those church members we designate as "mission partners" (the term that many churches now use in place of the older, rather loaded word

8. Christopher J. H. Wright, "Participatory Mission: The Mission of God's People Revealed in the Whole Bible Story," in *Four Views on the Church's Mission*, ed. Jason S. Sexton, Counterpoints: Bible and Theology (Grand Rapids: Zondervan, 2017), 90–91. Newbigin's distinction goes back to his early book *One Body, One Gospel, One World: The Christian Mission Today* (London: International Missionary Council, 1958).

missionaries). What does that make the rest of us? *Non*mission partners? Sleeping partners?

Now, of course, by *mission partners* we usually mean those who have been identified, appointed, and sent by the church and have gone overseas or into some kind of cross-cultural mission in their own country. Typically, they are then also financially paid by their fellow believers in their own or other churches, after "raising their own support," and often they work within some kind of support and accountability structure provided by a mission agency or society in cooperation with their sending church.

And we thank God for them! And we pray for them and provide for them in financial and other ways. In the words of the elder John about the itinerant "brothers and sisters" who were traveling "for the sake of the name" and needed the hospitality and support of local churches: "You will do well to send them on their journey in a manner worthy of God," so that "we may be fellow workers for the truth" (3 John 6–8 ESV—a beautiful description of missionaries and their supporters). And they can become wonderful ambassadors of reciprocal blessing between different parts of the global body of Christ (as such people were in New Testament times, like Epaphras, Epaphroditus, Phoebe, and others). So please do not misunderstand me: church-supported mission partners are a good and needed part of the way God's church goes about its missional obedience.

But to designate those we send overseas, *and them alone*, as "mission partners" does tend to imply that "mission" is what *they* do, rather than what *all* church members are engaged in, simply by being disciples of the Lord Jesus Christ. I wish we would qualify the term in some way, such as "*cross-cultural* mission partners" or "*international* mission partners" or "*funded* mission partners." And they may collectively constitute perhaps 1 or 2 percent of the church. So, however vital and important the work of church-supported cross-cultural mission partners is, they are only a tiny fraction of all the disciples of Jesus to whom the Great Commission is addressed.

Hugh Palmer, who was the rector (senior pastor) until May 2020 of All Souls Church, Langham Place, London (my home church), declared from the pulpit one Sunday, "This church sends out 1,500 mission partners every week" (that was the approximate membership of the church at the time). And then he added, "and a few of them are serving overseas." He was implying, of course, that the *whole congregation* every week is entering the "mission field" every time they walk out the doors of the church into the world outside. That's where they live and spend their time, in their everyday work and leisure. And that's where the mission field is: wherever faith meets unbelief, wherever the kingdom of God in a believer's life encounters the kingdom of this world. That is the front line of mission. And that could be next door as much as in the next continent. Wherever, whenever, however—every believer is called to live and work as a disciple of Jesus Christ, bearing witness in word and deed to the truth of the gospel, embodying as salt and light the presence, demands, and values of the kingdom of God.

So, then, the whole church's mission includes every church member. *But we have different callings and sendings.*

We need to distinguish between the *general* calling that all of us share as members of the church, on the one hand (i.e., the calling to be that people of God, redeemed in Christ, and indwelt by the Holy Spirit, as Paul says in Eph. 4:1 on the basis of all he has said in Eph. 1–3), and the *specific* giftings and callings, on the other hand, that God will lay on different ones according to his sovereign grace. In relation to our different marks of mission, for example, we can see both a general calling and specific gifting:

- *All* of us are to be ready to bear witness to our faith, while *some* are specifically gifted as evangelists.
- *All* of us are to "let the word of Christ dwell in [us] richly, teaching and admonishing one another" (Col. 3:16 ESV), while *some* are specifically gifted as teachers (Eph. 4:11; though not many, James 3:1).
- *All* of us are to be ready to do acts of compassion and kindness and speak up for what is just and right, while *some* are specifically called into professional work in politics or judicial advocacy or in tackling global poverty, hunger, and disease.

• *All* of us should live responsibly in our use and care of creation, while *some* are called, academically qualified, and professionally trained to pursue environmental biology and to do ecologically appropriate scientific research and advocacy.

Every church member can participate in his or her missional calling as part of God's people in the ordinary generality of seriously committed Christian living in the world, while God does also call and equip this one and that one for very specific missional callings that occupy their whole vocation or profession. We need to encourage, motivate, and honor both dimensions of mission.

God's whole mission is for God's whole church, and the whole church's mission includes every church member. That leads to a final point.

Every Church Member's Mission Includes the Whole of Life

We have to break the ingrained habit of thinking in two spheres—the secular and the sacred. It has become such a dominating paradigm in post-Enlightenment Western culture that we are scarcely conscious of it. It just seems to be the way things are. There is a "religious" part of life that God is interested in—church, Christian activities, worship and prayer, evangelism, and so on. And there is the rest of life, where most of us necessarily spend most of our time—the so-called secular world of work, family, leisure.

And we assume that the whole point of working in the secular sphere is only to give us some spare money and time to do whatever we can to "support" the sacred sphere, where the really keen Christians live in church-paid "full-time ministry." *They* are the ones doing "God's work." This "double think" infects so many areas of the church's life, including (especially) the popular concept of "ministry." It is still common for people to use that term exclusively to refer to work done in or for the church, paid by the church, including, of course, ordained pastoral ministry. And the impression is so often given that "a call to ministry" or "going into the ministry" means leaving "secular" work for the higher and more spiritual task of church-based ministry or some kind of church-supported mission work.[9]

This is a toxic and demoralizing dichotomy. The great majority of Christians are not (and should not be) in ordained pastoral ministry or cross-cultural missionary work or some other form of "full-time ministry." Yet when those callings are given some kind of elite status in the church, "ordinary Christians" easily fall into thinking that, on the one hand, what they have to spend *most* of their time doing (working in the "secular" world) has no value to God or for eternity; and on the other hand, they can only manage to give a *small amount* of their time to the one thing that they suppose God really cares about—so-called church work, or God's work. This is such a discouraging, disabling, demotivating, and frankly unbiblical way of looking at life.

John Stott was adamant in his opposition to this dichotomized way of thinking about ministry and mission. Biblically, the very concepts of ministry and mission should define and characterize the whole life of *every* disciple of Christ, in whatever way they exercise their gifts, abilities, and training, and however they fulfill their God-given desires and ambitions, even in the midst of all the circumstances in this fallen world that hinder and frustrate them. After making the same point about the different kinds of *diakonia* in Acts 6 (ministry of the word and ministry of "tables") that I referred to earlier,[10] Stott continues:

> It is a wonderful privilege to be a missionary or a pastor, *if God calls us to it*. But it is equally wonderful to be a Christian lawyer, industrialist, politician, manager, social worker, television script-writer, journalist, or home-maker, *if God calls us to it*. According to Romans

---

9. I remember hearing a newly appointed, ordained pastor being interviewed in a church service. Asked what had led him to be ordained, he said, "I used to be a math teacher. Then I realized that I loved Jesus more than math." I was distraught. What did that say to the schoolteachers in the congregation? That somehow sticking to teaching rather than getting ordained meant they loved Jesus less? Or that a pastor is showing their love for Jesus more than the Christian woman exhausting herself all week long as she pours out her energy and skills in a classroom for the sake of the children? This is the unbiblical spiritual damage of the "sacred-secular divide."

10. See n. 10 in chap. 6 above.

13:4 an official of the state . . . is just as much a "minister of God" (*diakonos theou*) as a pastor. . . .

There is a crying need for Christian men and women who see their daily work as their primary Christian ministry and who determine to penetrate their secular environment for Christ.[11]

To be crystal clear: John Stott was not diminishing the godly callings of ordained pastors within the church and of missionaries sent and supported by prayerful congregations, *nor am I*. In fact, Stott was hugely supportive (theologically, financially, and strategically) of both. Both are essential for the ministry of the church and its mission in the world. But neither the pastor nor the missionary is the sole occupant of the category of ministry or mission, when we think of those last two words with the kind of comprehensive breadth we find in the Bible. To put it bluntly, ministry is far too broad to be left entirely to "ministers" (meaning ordained pastors), and mission is far too extensive to be accomplished by "missionaries" alone. To exalt these church-paid roles as in some way a "higher calling" than the everyday work and service of all believers is to load them with far more than they can bear. "It is the hierarchy we have to reject, the pyramid we have to demolish," Stott concluded.[12]

To return, in conclusion, to our starting point: In the Great Commission, which stands at the central climax of the great story, Jesus begins by making the vast, cosmic claim that he is Lord of his whole creation. That must include his lordship over all areas of life on planet earth. Jesus is Lord of the workplace and the family; Lord of the streets and the skies; Lord of schools and slums; Lord of hospitals and housing; Lord of governments, business, academia, sport, and culture; Lord of all time and space; Lord of heaven and earth. There

---

11. John Stott, *The Contemporary Christian* (Downers Grove, IL: InterVarsity, 1992), 142 (italics original). It was this conviction that led Stott to found the London Institute for Contemporary Christianity, with a view toward equipping lay Christians in their wide range of vocations and professions to live as "whole-life disciples" by bringing a thoroughly biblical worldview to their working lives. The institute continues to battle the "secular-sacred divide" in its publications, as can be seen, for example, in Mark Greene, *The Great Divide* (London: London Institute for Contemporary Christianity, 2021), https://licc.org.uk/ourresources/the-great-divide/.

12. Stott, *The Contemporary Christian*, 142.

is no place on earth where our lives can be lived or our work can be done *outside* the governing authority of the Lord Jesus Christ. That means that the missional mandate of being disciples and making disciples is similarly ubiquitous—wherever Jesus is Lord. And that means everywhere.

Mission is not an agenda for a specialized task force. Mission is not a project to be completed by agencies equipped with every tool of management at their disposal. Mission is not an exotic vocation reserved for special people who are appointed, trained, sent, and paid to "do it for the rest of us."

Mission is the mode of existence for the whole life of every member of God's whole church.

May God help all of us and our churches to live out the implications of that reality.

For God's glory.

Scripture Index

Old Testament

Genesis

1 73, 112, 123, 126
1–2 17, 18
1–11 2
1:1 61, 108
1:20–21 116
1:22 115
1:24–31 116
1:26–28 17, 116–17
1:27 20
1:28 115
1:29–30 116
1:30 116
2 73, 118, 126
2:7 116
2:15 17, 116, 118
2:18–25 20
3 18–19, 55n10, 120
3:6 20
3:15 21, 25n11
3:17 20, 129
4–11 21
5:29 22
6:17 116

7:15 116
7:22 116
9:10 116
10 110
11 22
12 22
12:1–3 142
12:3 22
15 22
17 22
18 22
18:18 22
18:18–19 143
18:19 143, 143n2
18:25 32
22:18 22, 143
26:4 22
26:4–5 143
28:14 22, 143

Exodus

3:8–10 72n12
4:22 24
19:3–6 41
19:4–6 10, 24
19:6 119

34:6–7 91
34:6–8 70

Leviticus

10:10–11 83n8
25:23 24

Deuteronomy

2 110
4:1–14 83
4:6–8 96
4:15–20 115
4:32–39 58
4:39 29, 63, 95, 109
6:1–9 83
6:4–9 58
6:20–25 83
8:1 94
10:12–19 95
10:14 113
10:17–19 95
15:4–5 99
15:5 99n9
32:8 110
33:10 83n8

1 Kings

12:7 118

Job

29 32
31:26–28 115

Psalms

8 18
19 18
19:1 124
19:1–4 112, 123
24:1 17, 74, 113, 123
25:4–5 83
25:8–9 83
50:6 112
50:12 123
65:9–12 112
96 44
96–99 71
96:1–3 76
96:9 114
96:10–13 32, 132
96:13 122
97:1–2 91
97:2 70
98 44
101:1 91
104 18, 112, 117
104:14–30 116
104:25–26 121
104:27–30 112
104:29–30 116
104:31 123
115:16 17, 115
119:99 83
145:9 91, 117, 125
145:10 121
145:13 117, 125
145:13–17 125
145:16 117
145:17 91, 117, 125
145:21 121

148 18
148:7–13 121

Proverbs

12:10 125, 126
14:31 126
17:5 126
19:17 126
29:7 105, 125

Isaiah

6:3 123
11:6–9 131
32:1 131
32:15–20 131
35 131
43:8–10 30
52:7 76
58:6–8 97
58:10 97
60:1–3 97
61:8 91
64:1 139
65:17 131
65:17–25 34, 132
66:1 114

Jeremiah

29 8
29:7 73

Hosea

4:1–6 83n8

Micah

6:8 92

Zechariah

7:9 92

Malachi

2:1–9 83n8

New Testament

Matthew

4:1–11 94n6
5:6 91
5:7 92
5:13–16 72
5:16 96
5:43–48 103
6:1–4 91
6:33 92
7:21–27 89
16:18 63
23:23 92
25 126
28:16–17 109
28:16–20 29
28:18 109, 137
28:18–19 143
28:18–20 60, 61
28:19–20 82
28:20 87, 89, 99n9

Mark

1:1 76, 78n1
1:14–15 78n1

Luke

11:28 89
24:37–43 133
24:44–48 55
24:44–49 62
24:45–48 30
24:46 62
24:48 62

John

1:14 27
14:15 58
14:21 58
14:23 58
14:23–24 89
14:25–26 82
16:11 35
16:12–15 82, 83

17:6–8 83
17:13–18 47
17:20 43, 144n4
21 133

Acts

1:1–11 30
2:45 98
2:47 98
4:32–35 99
4:34 99
6 101, 150
6:1 100n10
6:2 99–100n10
6:4 100n10
10:38 70
11:27–30 99
12:25 100
13 99
13:1–3 100
13:17–22 35
14:17 112
17:24–26 110
18:27–28 85
19:1–7 84
20:20 84
20:27 36, 48, 65, 84
26:17–18 48

Romans

1:1 77
1:1–4 78n1
1:5 30, 58, 89
1:18–32 115
1:20 112
1:20–21 124
3:23 130
4 41
4:1–25 78n1
6:3–4 79
8 33, 129, 133, 134n3
8:18–25 133
8:20 130
8:21 130
8:23 133
9–11 41

13:1–7 101
13:3b 104n14
13:4 150–51
15:4 41
15:18–19 89
15:25 101
15:27 101
16:26 30, 58, 89

1 Corinthians

3:6–9 85
3:9 66
3:10 72n12
10 41
10:26 70, 74
15:3–4 56
15:3–5 78n1
15:20 35
15:44 133
16:1–4 101

2 Corinthians

4:6 96
5:14–17 2n2, 36
5:17 46
5:19 78n1
6:1 46, 66
8 101
8:13–14 101
9:13 89

Galatians

2:1–10 101
2:10 100
2:20 45
3:8 41, 142
3:26–29 79
3:29 41
6:10 103

Ephesians

1 28
1–3 148

1:9–10 35, 48, 59, 65
1:10 61, 130, 137
1:13–14 44
2–3 41
2:4–6 35
2:10 72
2:14–18 78n1
2:19–22 47
3:6 131
4:1 148
4:11 148

Philippians

3:9 43
3:20 45
3:21 133

Colossians

1:9 49, 65, 82
1:9–11 48
1:10 49
1:11 49
1:15–20 61, 70, 131, 136,
  137
1:15–23 74
1:20 78n1, 137
1:21 137
1:22 137
2:11–12 78
2:15 78n1
2:20–3:4 35
3:1–14 45
3:16 148

1 Thessalonians

1:2–3 58
1:9–10 48
2:1–2 101
2:14 20n8
6:17–19 105

2 Thessalonians

1:7–9 32
1:8 89

2 Timothy

1:13–14 84
2:1–2 84
3:15–17 41
3:16–17 42

Titus

1:1 x, 9, 103
1:5 104
1:12 9, 103
1:16 104n14
2 104n13
2:1–15 84
2:4 104n14
2:5 104
2:7 104n14
2:9–10 104
2:11–14 104
2:12–14 104
2:14 72, 88
3:1 72, 104n14
3:4–8 104
3:5–6 104
3:8 72, 88, 104, 104n14
3:14 72, 88, 104n14

Hebrews

1 29
2:14–15 78n1

5:9 89
11 42
11:1 44

James

2:14–17 105
2:14–26 89
3:1 148

1 Peter

2:9–12 41
2:24 78n1
4:17 89

2 Peter

3:3–4 134
3:6–7 135
3:10–12 135
3:10–13 134
3:13 135

1 John

2:3 89
2:20–27 82
3:2 133
3:17–18 105
3:21–24 89
5:1–3 89

3 John

6–8 147

Revelation

1 29
1:5 35, 54, 73
4–7 29
5:6 70
5:10 119
5:13 122
6:12–7:17 44
6:17 43
7:9 25
20 35
21 35n14
21–22 2, 34, 114, 132,
      135, 139
21:1 61, 108
21:3 34, 139
21:4–5 33
21:5 31
21:8 46
21:22 34
22:3–4 34
22:15 46

Printed in the USA
CPSIA information can be obtained
at www.ICGtesting.com
LVHW042203210724
786131LV00027B/236